Irises

Irises

A Practical Gardening Guide

Karen Glasgow

Photographs by Yvonne Cave

Timber Press
Portland, Oregon

Unfortunately, Karen Glasgow died before this book went into production, and the publishers have appreciated the assistance of the following people with editing and checking of the text and sourcing photographs: Marion Ball, President of the New Zealand Iris Society Inc., Hilmary Catton and Isobel Simpson, Hec Collins and Robert McKenzie.

The publishers are grateful also to Jocelyn Bell for allowing them to reproduce passages from *The Iris and its Culture* by Jean Stevens, and to Hilmary Catton, for her contribution to the text on pests and diseases.

Most photographs were provided by Yvonne Cave. Other photographers whose work is included are Gil Hanly, pp. 8, 16, 22 (left); Jack Hobbs, pp. 10 (right), 15 (left and right), 18, 19 (top), 39 (bottom right), 62, 71 (top), 82; Hec Collins, 39 (top) pp. 54 (right), 55 (left), 57 (bottom), 68 (top and bottom), 72. Photographs were also provided by the New Zealand Iris Society, pp. 9 (left), 38 (top right), 41, 54 (left), 55 (right), 73; and the Auckland Regional Botanic Gardens, pp. 28, 34, 79 (bottom), 85 (bottom).

First published in North America in 1997 by
Timber Press, Inc.
The Haseltine Building
133 S.W. Second Avenue, Suite 450
Portland, Oregon 97204, U.S.A.
1-800-327-5680 (U.S.A. and Canada only)

ISBN 0-88192-373-7

A CIP record for this book is available from the Library of Congress.

Cover design: Christine Hansen
Cover photograph and opposite title page: *Iris sibirica* (Yvonne Cave)
Typesetting and production: Kate Greenaway
Printed in Singapore

Contents

Iris:
the year-round flower

Irises are magnificent garden plants. They come in an infinite range of colours, as one would expect of a flower reputedly named for the rainbow goddess. They are bright and clear, soft and muted, mysterious in exotic dark colours, spotted, speckled, or striped in odd and unusual ways. Wherever they are in a garden, they command attention.

They come, too, in all sizes, from miniatures a few centimetres high to giants of 2 m and more. The variety of colour and size is such that they can be used in any number of places in the garden. There are irises for hot sunny beds, cool shady borders and in-between areas of dappled shade, for bone-dry areas and boggy situations. If all that is not enough, there are few months in the year when it is not possible to find an iris adding colour and grace to the season. A calendar can be drawn up, with very little stretching here and there, to provide flowers for every month of the year. The main flush of flowering is in the spring and early summer, but winter has its special beauties, and the seasons are linked by varieties that flower in-between.

However, there are still many gardeners who maintain that the season for irises is too short, that they prefer to use the space for longer-flowering plants. These people are only aware of the brightly coloured Tall Bearded irises, which flower over a period of roughly six weeks — shorter, certainly, than that of roses or dahlias but quite as long as the average herbaceous plant. The bloom season of Tall Bearded irises can be extended by selecting early, mid- and late-season flowering varieties. In this way the gardener may enjoy uninterrupted bloom for more than two months. Reblooming Tall Bearded irises are now readily available and will, if fertilised and watered, perform again in the late summer or autumn. Hybrids of species such as Spurias, Siberians, Louisianas and the Japanese also flower at staggered intervals and will prolong the bloom season.

While the splendid early summer pageant of the Tall Bearded irises is at its height, and before the subtler tones of the Japanese irises begin their show, the Spurias make their entrance. These are the statuesque beauties from the back of the border. Their colour range is not as extensive as that of the Tall Beardeds but the vibrant yellows, clear whites and rich browns of the new hybrids add another quality to the picture.

Opposite: Tall Bearded 'Leda's Lover'

The flowers are firmer and more solid, so that the rich colours have an almost enamel smoothness, polished and substantial. Their value for background planting cannot be over-estimated.

At the same time, the smaller Siberian irises come into bloom. The dominant colour among them is blue, in every conceivable gradation from the palest silver-blue through to rich dark blues and purples. As well there are good whites and interesting wine shades, all equally floriferous. The latest attempts of the hybridisers to produce a yellow Siberian are beginning to show results and some flowers with a distinctly cream-yellow tinge are obtainable.

Then there are the water irises, which again overlap with the Tall Beardeds and do not necessarily need water to flourish. Any rich border soil with plenty of compost suits them admirably, but needless to say they do need ample watering and plenty of sun. Japanese irises flower in late spring, sometimes even carrying over into mid-summer with an odd flower or two, following on the Tall Bearded show; they are, however, at their best in early summer. Their flowers contrast completely with the Tall Beardeds. They lie in a horizontal rather than a vertical plane, the standards

Tall Bearded irises make a splendid show in early summer

Spuria 'Betty Cooper'   A group of Siberians beside water

hardly erect at all, and the colour range of blue, white, pale pink, rose, mauve and plum shades adds a different dimension to the spectrum of iris colours.

Accompanying these are the wandering irises from the swamps of Florida and the Mississippi delta, the Louisianas. They have a long flowering season, often preceding the Tall Beardeds and accompanying the later water irises. The colours are clear and some of the newer varieties are quite exotic. The so-called Abbeville Reds, the earliest cultivated, and named for the district in which they were first discovered, are perhaps the nearest to red to be found in the iris family. They are a strong red-brown leaning heavily towards red with an orange tinge.

All these are taller members of the genus, but there are many rewarding dwarf species and varieties. There are the small counterparts of the Tall Beardeds — the Miniature Dwarf Beardeds, the Dwarf Beardeds, the Median and the Table irises, which are all daintier versions of their tall cousins. With these we add another two months to the beginning of the bearded irises' flowering season, as in the right situation the first dwarfs may flower in early spring or even, in the choicest warm corner, in late winter. They are ideal for the rock garden or as a border to a rock path into which they will happily creep. However, they do need rather more care and attention as they seem to use up the available soil nutrients more rapidly than the taller varieties.

At the same time as the Dwarf Beardeds are inching into flower, the bulbous Dutch irises are beginning to show colour. This race of free-flowering hybrids have the winter-flowering Algerian iris, *I. tingitana*, in their ancestry. The Spanish iris (*I. xiphium*) and Dutch irises come in a range of colours — yellows, blues, whites, brown shades and yellow bicolours; some flower with the early Dwarf Beardeds and continue for a long season. They are commercially grown as cut flowers and are in great demand.

I. tingitana is probably the most spectacular, and the most temperamental, of the bulbous irises. It increases rapidly, forming clumps of tall, graceful silver leaves, which make a shining patch in the winter garden. If they condescend to flower, the beautiful pale blue flowers on tall stems may appear in some districts in mid-winter, a most unexpected sight at this time of year, but they are as temperamental as they are lovely. Various treatments have been suggested to induce them to flower. A good summer baking would seem to be indicated, such as their North African homeland provides. Throw them on the shed roof for summer; spread them out in a hot dry place; or, as has been recorded, throw them over a fence onto a rubbish heap, where they will thrive. Whether they flower or not, a few bulbs are worth growing if only for the leaves.

Then there are the smaller bulbous irises. To start the season off, in unison with *I. tingitana*, are the Reticulata irises, whose netted bulbs give rise to the group's name. These little beauties, some 15 cm tall, begin to flower in mid-winter, the earliest often being *I. histrioides*, a lovely little free-flowering bright blue species. Its close relative

I. reticulata follows on with its rich purple-blue flowers. They are comparatively easy to grow in free-draining, reasonably good soil and should be given a little bulb fertiliser after flowering. Another necessity to keep them unblemished is plenty of slug bait.

Dwarf Bearded 'Sea Holly'

Dutch irises

10

I. reticulata

At the same time as we are anticipating the rich flowers of *I. tingitana*, another smaller, more floriferous plant, *I. unguicularis*, is delighting us with its succession of flowers in all shades of blue from very pale hues, through lavender to sky-blue, bright blue-purple and vibrant purple; there is also a white form, 'Alba', rather less compact and taller with a delightful sulphur reverse to the petals. Sometimes this form produces its first blooms in early autumn before it is joined by the others, so that by mid-winter there is a continuing supply of dainty blooms. They have a sweet fragrance and it only needs a few flowers to scent a room in winter.

The Evansia or crested irises, which flower from late winter to early summer, are different again. In place of a beard the flowers have a coxcomb crest along the median ridge of the falls. There are species from northeast America, Japan and China. They are essentially woodland plants that thrive in light shade, and some species make an excellent ground-cover under deciduous trees.

Also flowering in spring are the Pacific Coast irises, which range from Washington State to northern California in light woodland. The smallest and daintiest species, *I. innominata*, is the most difficult but is well worth a place in light shade with its many flowers in all shades of yellow, tan, blue and white. Its larger relatives are easier to please and colonise happily under deciduous trees, where they display a lively show from early spring onwards. Both *I. tenax* and *I. douglasiana* hybridise freely with the rest of the family, giving interesting colour combinations that are free-flowering for a long period.

There is a wide range of irises to grace the garden throughout the year, many more than are mentioned here but which are discussed later. Some of them, if you are skilful enough to persuade them to grow and flower for you, are among the choicest plants in the world and a triumphant addition to the iris collection.

11

The genus *Iris*

Irises are a diverse genus of around three hundred species, but extensive hybridisation has given rise to many more gardens forms. They belong to the family Iridaceae, which contains a host of other popular garden plants, such as gladioli and freesias. Many members of this family come from the southern hemisphere, in particular South Africa. However, the true irises are confined to the northern hemisphere.

Classification of the *Iris* genus is indeed a difficult task and botanists have still to reach a consensus on this. This is partly because of the number and diversity of species, the large number of forms and natural hybrids, and because some species are still poorly known. Thus in some books one species may be relegated to a variety of another species, or the Junos and Xiphiums may be considered distinct genera in their own right. Only time and further study will solve these problems.

As far as gardeners are concerned, irises can be divided into two main groups — rhizomatous and bulbous — depending on the type of storage organ. All bearded irises are rhizomatous, but beardless irises may be of either type.

The rootstock

The rhizomes creep horizontally at or just below the soil surface and may be large and fleshy, as in bearded irises. There are evergreen and deciduous rhizomatous species. A few irises, such as *I. cristata*, produce spreading underground stems (or stolons) in addition to rhizomes.

Rhizomatous irises can be divided into three groups — bearded, beardless and crested — based on floral characteristics. Botanically, these are subdivided into further groups (or series) of related species and hybrid races, such as the various bearded groups, Pacific Coast irises (series Californicae) and Siberian irises (series Sibiricae).

Bulbous irises make up a smaller group but are no less desirable, and the Dutch, English and Spanish irises are well-known florists' flowers. They produce true bulbs, to which they die back after flowering, coming back into growth in autumn or spring, depending on the species. Juno irises also produce fleshy storage roots in addition to the bulbs. Virtually all bulbous irises have beardless flowers. There are three groups of bulbous irises: Reticulatas, Junos and Xiphiums. Some are more challenging than others, but all are well worth growing.

It is not feasible to lay down any general rules for the cultivation of irises. They have only one thing in common: they are all inhabitants of the northern hemisphere.

Opposite: Tall Bearded 'Dunaverty'

The many species and forms of *Iris* extend from Europe and North Africa, across Asia to North America, and are native to a diverse range of habitats and climates. It is thus more practical to include directions for cultivation with the discussions of the different groups.

The flower

Their characteristic and distinctive flowers make irises instantly recognisable. Although they vary between the different groups, all iris flowers have the same basic structure. The perianth (or petals) consists of six segments that arise from a perianth tube, at the base of which is the ovary. The base of the flower — the perianth tube, ovary and individual flower stalk — is usually enclosed within a green bract-like spathe. The three outermost perianth segments are known as falls and are either held horizontally or droop at various angles. The three inner segments are called standards and are usually held erect, but they can be horizontal or occasionally drooping. The standards may be large and broad, as in bearded irises, or very small and bristle-like, as in *I. setosa*.

At the top of the falls, bearded irises have a central line of short bristly hairs, which are, of course, absent in the beardless irises and in almost all bulbous irises. In their place, crested irises have a ridge or crest. The falls of beardless irises usually have a large, often bright yellow, signal patch (or nectar guide) in this position.

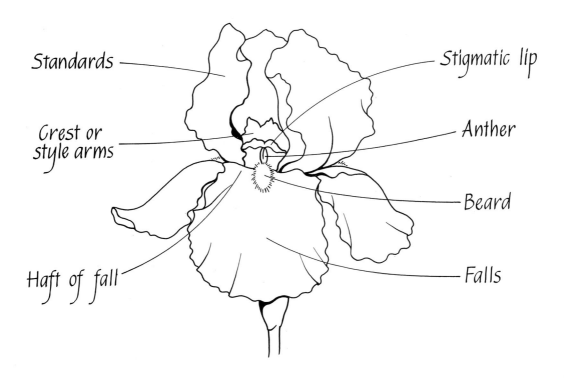

Structure of the iris flower

14

This specimen of 'Lady Friend' clearly shows the beard at the top of the falls.

I. pseudacorus 'Variegata' is commonly grown for its striking foliage.

Between each standard and fall is the unusual style arm, which arches over the base (or haft) of the falls and the pollen-bearing anther. On the underside of each arm near the tip is the stigmatic surface, on which pollen adheres prior to fertilisation. The tip of the style — the style crest — is often colourful and petal-like and contributes to the beauty of the flowers.

The flowers come in all shades except true reds, which together with the huge range of intricate markings and colour combinations adds to the diversity within the genus.

The foliage

The typically sword-like foliage is produced in fans and varies considerably in size and colour. It may be flat or deeply channelled and V-shaped. In some species the leaves have arching tips. In one or two smaller species the foliage is rather grass-like. In many species it is glaucous or silvery. There are also a number of variegated forms, such as *I. pseudacorus* 'Variegata' and *I. laevigata* 'Variegata'.

Irises, therefore, have much more to offer gardeners than simply beautiful flowers. Through their foliage and form they can be attractive features in any garden, even when not in flower, so when planning your garden this should not be overlooked.

Irises in the garden

In the border

Irises are beautiful and versatile garden plants. So many and varied are the species and cultivars that some can be found for every situation and aspect, and most of them will grow with little attention. Their demands, though simple, need to receive some consideration. Some species require full sun to give of their best; others prefer some shade. Some require damp situations, which are death to others of their relatives. Some are happy in dry poorish soil; others prefer it rich and moist. Once their tastes are known and their requirements met, they will provide beauty for many years.

Some of the species are most spectacular when given space to themselves. The Tall Bearded irises are magnificent when grown alone so as to show off the variety and range of their colours. However, their decorative foliage becomes monotonous when flowering is over, and the beauty of the fans is much better appreciated as an accent in a mixed border. The Spuria irises, too, are most handsome in a separate planting. The tall spiring foliage and the flower-topped stalks make an impressive sight. But as background plants in a border or group of herbaceous plants, they provide a contrast to lower and more compact plants. When topped by bright spires of flowers, they lift the border up and beyond.

Because of the various likes and dislikes of the different types it is not always very satisfactory or even possible to grow them all together. Today's smaller gardens mean that careful consideration has to be given to planning if we wish to grow as many as possible of the irises available to us. Depending on how much space is at your disposal and how the site lies to the sun, if it is open to wind or is liable to frost, the number and type of irises grown will be limited by these factors. If you have a summer garden facing north and west, a few Tall Bearded irises will give a month to six weeks of vibrant colour, will require little watering and can be left alone for several years, although if they increase vigorously, they may need thinning at the end of two years. Some varieties are much more vigorous than others and can take over a surprising amount of ground quite rapidly.

If the border is wide enough to allow for the provision of pockets of different types of soil, several plants of Spuria irises will add much interest and contrast with the Tall Bearded forms. The Spurias recommended for these back-border positions are the tall varieties, which respond well to the use of organic manure but do not like lime. As

Opposite: A massed border planting of Tall Bearded irises shows the variety and range of colours.

This mass planting of 'Madonna' is effective in a border.

the Tall Beardeds need lime and if given too rich a soil tend to produce leaf rather than flowers, it pays to keep them somewhat apart, although both types are tolerant to some extent of each other's diet.

A small Spuria to introduce into the front of the border is *I. sintenisii*. This is a very showy little iris, evergreen and tufted, whose blue and white flowers show gaily across the garden. An advantage is that it is tolerant of limey soils so it can be grown in proximity to bearded irises. Once established, it is very drought-resistant, as its bearded neighbours are.

I. tectorum, of the Evansia group, is another useful iris in a border. Its much lighter yellow-green fans show up well and the light blue flowers lighten the overall effect. It prefers a well-drained sunny site with a loose friable soil, rich in organic matter. It is easy enough to provide for its needs without upsetting its neighbours. It seems almost indifferent to lime, although it does appear to respond to a light dressing early in winter.

The graceful Siberian irises, like swarms of butterflies, must be included in an iris potpourri. They are valuable plants in the border, providing shades of blue, white and wine at a time when these colours are appreciated. Their soil requirements are much the same as those of the Spurias, with the same dislike of lime. As they come into flower when the bearded irises are almost at the end of their display, they take their place in the border and complement the beauty of their dignified background cousins, the tall Spurias

The vibrant yellow of 'Foxfire' is reinforced by the surrounding *Euphorbia epithymoides*.

Irises add colour and stately form to this cottage-style garden.

In water and bog gardens

Without doubt, some of the most spectacular and easy-to-grow beardless irises are those best suited to the water garden and its boggy margins. They can be tall, robust roamers and ideal in the large garden. Generally they dislike lime and require rich acid conditions with plentiful water in their growing season and a drier dormant period.

The truly aquatic species carry their own 'water mark' in the form of dark blotches in the veins of the leaf. The species *I. laevigata* is one such and is better grown in water all year round. It is the first of these water irises to flower in the spring. Even the smallest pool can usually support at least one laevigata in a tub.

The yellow water flag of Europe, *I. pseudacorus*, is another that will grow and bloom in year-round water. It is a tough survivor that has colonised vast tracts along streams and water meadows. Some gardeners prefer to keep it in tubs to check its wanderlust. The spent bloom stalks should be removed to prevent the spread of seed.

Others that cover the damp margins of the large pond are the Louisianas. Their modern hybrids come in a stunning range of colours and blends. Bloom from early, mid- and late-flowering varieties will further extend their season. Louisianas need

I. pseudacorus 'Variegata' looks wonderful growing on the edge of a pond.

Japanese irises thrive in waterside conditions.

ample moisture and food in the spring and autumn, and can withstand summer's drought provided the large rhizomes have a covering of mulch to protect them from the sun. They also need a warm and humid climate to perform well.

I. ensata and its hybrid strains has been cultivated in Japan for more than five hundred years and much ceremony and mystique has grown around their bloom and display. Today's hybrids are available in single with three petals, like the type, double with six petals, or the 'dinner plate' size of the triple, peony types. The colours range from whites through to purples, blues, plums and pinks with contrasting bands of colour or veins. They are late-flowering irises and will bloom well into midsummer in some areas. Spring and summer moisture is essential and they must be dry in winter. They are gross feeders and very fond of a dressing of cow manure.

For aesthetic reasons some gardeners like to place these irises in water during the flowering period. They must be taken out after the bloom season has finished.

Species lovers could also plant the Americans *I. versicolor* and *I. virginica* on the damp margins of the pool. Easy and graceful, they make a handsome addition to the water-garden scene.

In rock gardens

There are so many small irises that would be lost in the general border that a special bed or a small rock garden where each plant can have its own little patch are better settings. The rock garden is most suitable as it easily allows for pockets of different soil types to suit each plant. Some of the most desirable of these little irises belong to the Reticulata group of bulbous irises, only a few centimetres high, in colours ranging from pale blue through to darker and bright blues to the red-purple *I. reticulata* itself. They come into flower in mid-winter and make a gay display until the end of winter. Half a dozen bulbs set in a rockery, or in a container in the open garden, will provide pleasure in the late winter, for these fragile-looking flowers stand up well to the weather. It certainly pays to give them a sheltered sunny spot.

Another small iris I would never be without is *I. cretensis* (syn. *I. unguicularis* subsp. *cretensis*), the smallest of the Unguicularis series. It makes a tight grassy clump very like a grey wig when the leaves are ageing. These can be combed out with one's fingers. The jewel-like flowers emerge from the tangle, sapphire overlaid with purple and sporting a bright gold stripe on the falls. Their toughness gives the lie to their frail appearance as they appear in some of coldest weather of the year. Fill a pocket in full sun with gritty soil, not too rich, add a sprinkle of lime and tuck in the plant. In time

This Dwarf Bearded hybrid makes an excellent rock garden subject.

I. graminea is a beautifully scented Spuria.

it will cram itself into its space and, it seems, the tighter the mop, the more flowers it produces.

The smallest iris of them all is well worth persevering with, as the slugs agree. This is *I. minutoaurea*, which hails from Japan. Only 2–5 cm tall, it has grassy foliage that eventually grows to about 23 cm long but at flowering time it is very short. The flowers are a pale yellow, the standards primrose and the falls yellow with a fine brown median stripe. Unfortunately, it is a delicacy for the slug tribe, who often eat it out before the minute fan comes through the ground. A loose, not too rich, lime-free soil in full sun suits it best.

There is one more Spuria that is suitable for a rather larger pocket: this is *I. graminea*, with a purple-blue scented flower nestling in the leaves. The scent is variously described as that of greengages, apricots or even plums. Whatever it is, it is nice and the plant should be in every garden.

Dwarf Bearded irises also do well in rock-pockets, making a bright addition to the spring scene. And there are so many of them to choose from that there is sure to be something suitable for all gardens, however small the available space.

In woodland gardens

There are three dwarf treasures suitable for growing under trees: one from the woodlands of Japan, the other two from streamsides and light woods in North America. All are members of the Evansia group and need cool or lightly shaded places. Being woodland plants, they relish leaf mould and need it to protect their little rhizomes in summer. *I. gracilipes* is a fairy iris, with a lavender-blue bloom on wiry stems up to 30 cm in height. The grace, balance and proportions make this one of the daintiest flowers in the garden. There is a white form, too.

The other two sit closer to the ground — *I. lacustris* is 5–7.5 cm tall and *I. cristata* 10–15 cm. Both have flat little flowers of soft blue with white, gold-tipped crests. A well-covered clump is like a patch of sky fallen down. The tiny slender rhizomes must never be allowed to dry out, but they need good drainage and to be continuously supplied with lime-free leaf mould.

The tall Evansias are also admirably suited to the woodland garden. Except for *I. tectorum* and *I. milesii*, they prefer filtered shade and flourish particularly well in that untamed patch around large deciduous trees. When it was first introduced to the Mediterranean area of France, *I. japonica* became known as Il Perengrino for its wandering habits. Others of the family are more inclined to clump and will not spread as much and the reward is a succession of lavender and blue frilly blooms for up to two

I. gracilipes (left) and *I. cristata*, white form, are two irises suitable for woodland planting.

Siberians make an effective group at the edge of this woodland.

Evansias thrive in a woodland environment.

I. innominata grows well in part shade on the edge of a woodland garden.

months from late August until early summer. The handsome fans of glossy green leaves on top of sometimes tall canes are an attractive addition during winter months.

These are shallow-rooting plants and do not care for much fussy cultivation. All that is really necessary is to remove last season's dead canes, an annual sprinkling of an all-purpose fertiliser and some snail bait. Otherwise they can be left alone. Frost can damage the leaves and they prefer warmer districts.

The edges of this woodland garden can be planted with Pacific Coast irises. They too enjoy filtered light from deciduous trees and shelter from the summer sun. They strongly resent being watered in the heat of the day, and humid conditions can lead to a form of brown rot and collapse of the plant. The easiest form of propagation of this series is by growing them from seed.

The very desirable *I. verna* is another creature of the woodland. Native to the wooded areas of the Appalachian and Ozark Mountains in North America, it requires acid conditions and humusy soil. It will bloom in the early spring before the heavy leaf of the overhead trees is established.

I. foetidissima also likes shade. Its claim to beauty in most cases is in the brilliant red seeds. The variegated form will light up a dry and dreary corner. *I. foetidissima* is a rapid and prolific increaser and can colonise large areas if not kept in check. In some areas it has become a noxious weed.

English irises, the descendants of *I. latifolia*, will also tolerate more shade than others species. They are a late-flowering iris and the very last of the bulbous irises to bloom in early summer. They need to be kept fairly damp and like neutral to acid conditions.

In containers

Of all the species of irises, very few have been thought suitable for pot culture, perhaps because they are hungry feeders and soon exhaust the nutrients in an enclosed space. Gardening in containers has now become so popular that consideration should be given to those irises that will adapt to growing and blooming in pots. In this way the gardener with limited space can add variety to the seasonal display. Those irises needing protection from climatic changes can also be grown in pots and moved around. Lastly, containers are ideal for irises whose wandering habits make them a menace in the small garden.

The first species to come to mind are some of the water-loving irises. Even a small pool will hold several Japanese irises planted in large pots. The soil mix needs to be very rich, with lots of compost and cow manure if possible. Add no artificial fertiliser if there are fish in the pool. Soak the pot thoroughly before planting, and after the iris is well firmed in, cover the surface of the pot with some coarse gravel or small stones. Place in the pond so that the water level is 4–5 cm above the soil. After flowering, when the iris has begun to die down, remove from the tub and leave in a sheltered spot, such as under a hedge, for winter. In the spring, when the first shoots appear, repot if necessary; otherwise, scrape away the top 4–5 cm of soil and add fresh compost

These container-planted *I. laevigata* are easy to
manage in a water garden.

I. 'Sindpers', a hybrid Juno, is a good container subject.

and some manure as a boost.

I. laevigata can be grown in tubs in the same way but they do not need to be moved from the pool in winter. Just trim the tops back when they begin to die down. These varieties dislike lime. A new concrete tub needs to be 'seasoned' first before placing plants in it. Leave for up to twelve months and change the water several times.

The large and vigorous Louisianas can be kept in order in a tub. It should be a big one, and they may need to be repotted every season. The soil mix is the same, rich and lime-free. Louisianas should receive a thorough soaking every day in spring and summer. They are evergreen but late summer's leaves are inclined to be untidy. At this stage the tub could be moved out of sight.

Bearded irises may also be grown in tubs or containers. They are heavy feeders and will soon exhaust the mix. The most suitable for pot culture are the Miniature and Standard Dwarfs, which do well in troughs with companion plants that enjoy the same alkaline conditions. Tall Beardeds can grow up to a metre tall and will need to have a large container with extra good drainage holes. Add some coarse gravel or pumice and slow-release fertiliser to the potting mix, and before planting test the drainage. Pour a bucket of water into the pot and if it drains away in 30 seconds, the drainage is sharp enough.

Pacific Coast irises are also suitable for growing in pots, particularly the smaller, fine-leaved variety sold in some nurseries as *I. innominata*. The strain has been crossed now so many times that variation in colour and form is very wide. If grown from seed, sow directly into the chosen container with plenty of leaf mould and a little grit. Add a small amount of slow-release fertiliser. They require plenty of moisture in the spring, little in the summer, and must never be watered in the heat of the day. These irises grow in neat clumps and several plants would fit into a large pot.

The smaller of the Evansia species could well be grown in tubs in a shady situation. Use a similar mix to that recommended for Pacific Coast irises with the addition of well-rotted manure. They will need fresh soil every couple of years and the evergreen foliage, if protected from wind and frost, can be very attractive.

I. reticulata is another that does very well in a container. This is a good way of keeping track of the tiny bulbs and the pot can be brought inside when the plants are in bloom. However, they must be planted early and deeply (15 cm) so the pot has to be able to support that requirement. A light, neutral mix is preferred with a dressing of dried blood in spring.

I. bucharica and its relative *I. magnifica* are the easiest of the Junos to grow, and their culture is better managed if they are planted in deep buckets. They come into growth with the onset of the autumn rains, bloom in the early spring, and dry off as summer approaches. At this stage they are best put under the shelter of the eaves or somewhere very dry until they come into growth again. Occasionally the hybrid 'Sindpers' is available; treat this in the same way.

Irises that like to form clumps and do not like being disturbed for years, such as Siberians and Spurias, are unsuited to pot culture, but there are many other small species which, given the right mix and attention, would be ideal as pot plants.

I. reticulata 'Springtime' (left) and *I. innominata* are both suitable for containers.

Rhizomatous irises

Bearded irises

The bearded species have given rise to the mass of colourful cultivars that grace our gardens today. They are characterised by stout rhizomes that produce fans of rather broad, sword-shaped leaves and simple or branched stems carrying two or more flowers; in some of the smaller species, such as *I. pumila*, there is a single short-stemmed or stemless flower. The flowers of all species have well-developed falls and standards and a prominent beard in the centre of each fall. They range in height and size from over 1 m high to the Miniature Dwarfs as small as 5 cm tall.

Generally speaking, bearded irises are easy to grow. All they require is a well-drained open situation in full sun, although in areas where the winter is fairly dry it seems not to matter if there is less sun on the plants, provided the amount of sunshine increases as spring develops. A good summer baking will promote flowering. Raising the level of the bed will help to ensure drainage is adequate in heavy soils. The taller forms also require shelter from wind.

When preparing to plant, cultivate the plot as deeply as possible, adding garden compost or some well-rotted organic material. This must be well broken down or the plants tend to produce lush leaves and few flowers. Contrary to past ideas, bearded irises do like some nourishment and an application of a balanced fertiliser, such as a rose mixture, in both spring and autumn is desirable. Avoid fast-acting nitrogenous fertilisers and manures, as these will discourage flowering. Bearded irises prefer a neutral soil and during winter a light dressing of lime or dolomite should be applied to counteract any inclination to acidity in the soil. Watering should only be necessary for newly planted irises, which need to be well watered after planting so that the roots are well established before spring. The more dwarf the iris, the more it needs to be watered after re-planting. Reblooming hybrids may require watering, fertilising and dividing more frequently in order to maintain their vigour and encourage repeat flowering. After a dry winter, bearded irises should be watered before they bloom.

Bearded irises are best planted, or divided and replanted, in early summer immediately after flowering or in early autumn to allow time for good root development before the onset of winter. Make sure the rhizomes are kept clear of weeds and their own dying foliage, and if they are to be grown in a mixed border, take care that surrounding plants do not shade the iris bases too much.

Opposite: An award-winning Tall Bearded hybrid 'First Movement'.

Rhizome rots are probably the main problem with bearded irises, but leaf spot, rust and aphids may also attack them.

Bearded species

There appear not to be many wild species of bearded iris, but the true position is somewhat obscured because there are a number of hybrids, some of which are well established in semi-wild situations and are thought to be species. Many of these hybrids from different localities have been named, however they have little more claim to specific rank than any of the modern cultivars.

The first of the bearded irises to come into flower are those of the *I. germanica* group (the common flag or German iris). At one time they were thought to be the forebears of the modern Tall Bearded irises. However, many are now considered to be hybrids themselves between dwarf species and the larger European bearded irises and have been reduced to cultivar status. They also appear to be infertile. They have strong green foliage and tall stems 1 m or so high with blue-purple flowers about four weeks before the Tall Bearded irises.

It is not easy to distinguish *I. germanica* forms that have been described as species. 'Albicans' is a shortish plant with grey-green overwintering leaves with narrowed incurving tips. The stem has one to three terminal flowers. It is often unbranched but may have one sessile lateral flower-head. The sweetly scented flowers are either pure white or pale blue, produced from very blunt broad bracts that are green or purplish tinted in the lower half and papery transparent in the upper half. This species is frequently confused with 'Florentina' but is easy to distinguish because the bracts of 'Florentina' are almost wholly brown and papery at flowering time. As well, the lateral flowers are stemmed and the flowers themselves are not as pure white as 'Albicans'; the leaves are also greener in colour. 'Albicans' is a native of the Middle East. It is found widely in western Asia and parts of Europe and this has been explained by the fact that the Mohammedans treasured it for grave plantings and carried it with them on their journeys.

I. trojana, *I. cypriana* and *I. mesopotamica*, which appear to be closely related, are well worth growing where space permits. *I. cypriana* is a large pale blue-lilac species from Cyprus. During the quick growth of late spring its 1 m stems are unable to bear the weight of the fleshy buds and droop over but recover later as the stem becomes firmer in development. This is a very beautiful iris whose beauty is somewhat detracted from by this habit.

I. mesopotamica (syn. *I. ricardii*) is another of the germanica clan, probably not a true species, which is named from the area in which it is commonly found. The stems are 90–120 cm high with long side branches and large, rather floppy flowers of lavender-blue. It can be frost-tender in colder areas because of its tendency to produce winter growth.

I. trojana has a few features that make it a good garden plant. It is 60–70 cm in height with wide branching that has been of great value to the iris world. The sweetly scented flowers have lavender-blue standards and purplish blue falls, and the long narrow buds are stained purple. The rhizome has a tendency to make long unbranched forkings from the old stock, sometimes as much as 15 cm before branching again. This iris has been of the utmost value in the breeding world, together with *I. variegata*.

It is of interest that the 'neglecta' type of colouring, i.e. light blue standards and darker blue falls, can be gained by using *I. trojana* in hybridising.

I. pallida (syn. *I. dalmatica*) comes from southern Europe and is distinguished by the papery silvery white spathes sheathing the buds, quite unlike those of any other species. It is a tall plant with branched stems up to 1.2 m in height, short broad blue-green foliage and soft silvery blue-lilac flowers with a delicious scent; in the form 'Dalmatica' the colour is a lovely blue with no lilac or purple tonings. This is the iris that is grown in Italy as a crop for the production of orris root.

In *I. aphylla* the species name (meaning 'leafless') applies probably to the somewhat leafless-looking long branches of the flower stalk rather than to the fact that the plant is dormant and leafless in winter. It has a 15–30 cm stem that is branched from near the rhizome. The flowers vary from pale to dark purple or violet-blue. *I. aphylla* has been used extensively in hybridising, especially for Miniature Tall Beardeds, for its branching and slender stems.

I. lutescens (syn. *I. chamaeiris*) is a short-stemmed dwarf iris that occurs in dryish, grassy or rocky places, sometimes beneath pine trees, in northeastern Spain, southern France and Italy. The flower is often yellow or a combination of yellow and violet (or even violet or occasionally white). Not only is it very variable in colour but also in height, ranging between 5 cm and 30 cm tall at flowering time. Most of the forms are free-flowering and deliciously scented.

I. pallida

I. lutescens

I. suaveolens (syn. *I. mellita*) is a delightful little iris that has been grown for many years both in this form but more usually in the form *I. s.* var. *rubromarginata*, which is somewhat more dwarf than the type with noticeably red-margined sickle-shaped leaves. It is an attractive little imp with flowers of a strange shot-silk blend of bronze-brown and purple with a tiny white beard prominently blue-tipped. Each stem, from 10 cm high, carries one flower. A patch of it can be most attractive and unusual, but being a plant from the hills of Greece and the Mediterranean, it needs perfect drainage and a loose rich soil with added lime.

I. pumila is undoubtedly the best known of the smaller bearded irises and, in its various forms, covers a wide territory throughout central Asia and southern Europe to Russia. The true *I. pumila* has practically no stem, seldom more than 1 cm up to the base of the bracts. The plant relies on its perianth tube to hold the flowers above the base of the leaves. There is normally one flower and the colours range through every shade of blue, lilac, purple and yellow. *I. pumila* and its forms are not easy to grow as, after a good start for the first few years, they tend to dwindle away; even in a raised bed they do not seem to be co-operative for long. The soil must not contain too much nitrogen but should be lime-rich. *I. pumila* is well known as the ancestor of many Standard Dwarf Bearded hybrids. It introduced colour and pattern variations like spots and rays to this section.

I. reichenbachii closely resembles *I. suaveolens* and it has been sold as such or even as *I. pumila*. It is quite easy to grow but is not a particularly attractive species, the flowers being rather a muddy yellow, dirty purple or violet. It is native of southeastern Europe.

I. variegata is a small but important species from central and southeastern Europe.

Standard Dwarf Bearded 'Meadow Court'

I. reichenbachii

The flowers vary somewhat in the wild but the standards and style arms are always more or less yellow, the falls being yellow-toned, striped and flushed with red-brown or blackish brown. It is quite a spectacular little iris, usually about 20–45 cm in height when in flower, with two side branches. It has narrow ribbed foliage and is entirely deciduous, losing its leaves in autumn and not coming into growth until well into the spring.

It is to this gaudy little iris more than to any other species that we owe the wealth of loveliness that we find in modern Tall Bearded irises. It was from this species alone that every yellow tone and every colour combination requiring yellow was bred. It seems it is also to *I. variegata* that we owe today's true pink irises, all of which contain some *I. variegata* blood. It is a plant of light woodland, scrub and open stony places in southern Europe.

Hybrid bearded irises

The first of the hybrid bearded irises to take up the season are the Miniature Dwarf Beardeds (MDBs) derived from *I. pumila* and *I. lutescens*. There are many beautiful hybrids to choose from and, being almost stemless and only up to 20 cm tall, they are ideal for pockets in the rock garden or on the raised edges of a bed. If they are planted in sunny situations in well-cultivated soil, they quite quickly make sizeable clumps and produce a succession of two-flowered stems. Being so close to the ground they are in constant danger from slugs and snails, which must be heavily discouraged.

The next group is that of the Median irises, in which can be included the Standard Dwarf Beardeds (SDBs) and the Intermediate Beardeds. The former have branched stems 20–38 cm high with three or four flowers per stem, level with or above the leaves. There are beautiful hybrids available in this group, which come into flower at about the same time as the MDBs. They, too, make good rock-garden plants or edging plants.

The Intermediate Beardeds, bred from Tall Bearded irises and *I. pumila* with some help from *I. aphylla*, overlap the SDBs and Tall Beardeds in their flowering season and are intermediate in height between the two. They should have strong stems, good branching, two or more branches and at least six flowers. They are most elegant and attractive plants.

The two remaining groups of Median irises are the Miniature Tall Beardeds and the Border Beardeds. They are in the same height range, 40–70 cm, but the Border Beardeds have more robust flowers and thicker stems. They can be grown in more exposed places than the Tall Beardeds, otherwise cultivation is much the same for all these groups except that the miniatures seem to require more frequent shifting and more feeding as they wear out their sites rather more quickly than the others.

Mention the word iris to the average gardener and he or she at once conjures up a vision of the stately, richly coloured Modern Tall Bearded irises that are such a delight

Miniature Dwarf Bearded hybrids 'Irish Trick' (left) and 'Gingerbread Man'

Miniature Dwarf Bearded hybrids 'Mighty Mite' (left) and 'Gentle Grace'

to grow — and with good reason. They have been described as the extroverts of the iris world. The largest of the bearded irises, they rise in three parts to a flowery summit, in their best form gracefully balanced in sculptured perfection.

They are the last of the bearded irises to come into flower in late spring, carrying on in some areas well into summer. Their flowers are among the loveliest and showiest in the garden, and they come in every colour and combination of colours. They are self-coloured, two-toned, spotted, freckled, or dusted with contrasting colours; some have narrow edgings of a contrasting colour, others much wider, and to crown it all some have vivid orange, gold or red beards. The only colour missing is true red, which hybridisers are striving to achieve. We have wine-reds, reddish browns and oranges, but the true red still eludes the experts.

The two European species that contributed most to the development of Modern Tall Bearded irises were *I. pallida* and *I. variegata. I. pallida* had height but branching was almost non-existent, the flowers being bunched near the top of the spike on 5 cm side branches, resulting in a great mass of petals when the flowers were fully developed. *I. variegata* was also short in stature with small lateral stems and so did little to improve the growth habit of any hybrids derived from it.

It was not until Dr Michael Foster, who was deeply interested in the genus, imported some of the Middle Eastern species into England that appreciable progress was made. The first to be imported were *I. trojana* and *I. cypriana*, followed later by *I. mesopotamica.*

Median irises (clockwise from top left): 'Wyona Evening', 'Flash Dance', 'Peachy Face' and 'Florizel'

Tall Beardeds 'Basic Black' (top), 'Catalyst' (above left) and 'Good Bye Heart'

I. trojana vastly improved the branching of the *I. pallida* hybrids. Branching was again improved when *I. mesopotamica* was introduced into the programme. Unfortunately, its tendency to winter growth militated against the success of the hybrids in the English climate, although it has little effect in the southern hemisphere.

In the 1940s and 1950s there was a tremendous upsurge of interest in the United States in the hybridising of bearded irises. The first result of this was a flood of Tall Bearded irises in a wide range of bright and attractive colours and distinctly different in the size and shape of the flowers. The early introductions tended to be leggy, with widely spaced branches, or top heavy with drooping falls on swan-necking stems. These faults were quickly improved: the swan necks were eliminated and straight, strong stems with closer branching were developed, together with flowers that were longer-lived, more weather-tolerant and which had broader falls for greater impact. They soon became popular among gardeners and this interest widened considerably until bearded irises were evident in parks and public gardens as well as in private gardens.

Aril irises

These are the bearded species from the semi-arid lands of the Middle East and Central Asia, and they include the Oncocyclus and Regelia sections. Aril irises are distinctive in that the seeds have a white or cream appendage at one end. Coming, as they do, from regions experiencing hot dry summers, they are not easy to grow in temperate climates. However, if a suitable spot can be found under the eaves of the house and facing into the sun, a certain amount of success can be achieved. They come into growth in autumn and flower in early spring before sitting dormant over summer. It is most important to keep them dry in summer and see that they have good drainage. Many are also intolerant of cold winters.

Arilbred irises are hybrids between the Aril irises and the Tall Beardeds and are easier to grow in situations where the Modern Tall Beardeds do well. Their Aril ancestry adds an interesting and exotic touch to the flowers. They also require a well-drained soil and replanting every two years is advisable, as they tend to be heavy feeders.

ONCOCYCLUS IRISES. This section contains the most beautiful, the strangest and the most difficult members of the whole genus. It is everyone's ambition to grow one of them successfully, just once; few of us ever succeed. They are native to areas of southern Europe and the Middle East. For the most part they are xerophytic plants adapted to life in excessively dry conditions. Summers tend to be hot and dry coupled with a relatively dry, cool winter, when the plants may be tucked beneath a blanket of snow so that they spend the winter more or less in a state of dormancy. Oncocyclus species generally have a long dormant period during the summer. In the autumn when the soil temperature is still reasonably high some root growth will begin, possibly also some leaf growth. Falling temperatures from then on will slow growth right down and there will be little movement until the spring.

The essential ingredient for the successful culture of these irises is protection, by some means, from excessive summer and autumn moisture, which is likely to cause rhizome rot. Plenty of light and good air circulation are also necessary. A reasonably good soil containing lime suits them best and they should have perfect drainage, as

40

I. susiana

they are plants of rocky places with an unlimited root run. However, even given all these requirements, success is by no means certain — or even likely!

Botanically the Oncocyclus group is fairly easily defined. They are rhizomatous and have only one flower to a stem. The flowers have lush velvety beards and the falls are strongly reflexed. Both the falls and standards are intricately marked, giving the flowers a breathtaking beauty. The seeds have a conspicuous, often whitish, aril that is usually nearly as large as the body of the seed itself.

I. susiana, the mourning iris, is the best known of the Oncocyclus section, although it seems to be gradually disappearing from gardens and is almost impossible to obtain. An attempt was made some years ago to produce fresh stock by means of meristem culture, but this failed to eliminate the virus that is so weakening the remaining specimens. *I. susiana* has been in cultivation for at least four hundred years. It is reported to have been sent to Vienna in 1573 by the then Austrian ambassador to Turkey and from there reached other places in Europe. In all these years it has never been found in the wild. It has been propagated vegetatively ever since and the plant we have today is probably the same clone as that imported from so long ago. This seems almost incredible and is a possible explanation for the decreasing vigour of today's plants, in this part of the world at any rate.

I. susiana is perhaps the dullest coloured of the large species. The large flower is heavily veined with deep purple on a greyish ground. The signal patch is rich velvety, ruby-toned black crowned by a wide, thick, deep bronze-purple beard. The falls have the convex-rounded form typical of the larger species, with colour effects slightly darker than in the standards. The style arms are dark ruby-purple with no veining.

41

A Regelio-cyclus iris, a hybrid between Regelia and
Oncocyclus groups

The leaves are slightly glaucous and about 2.5 cm wide. The flower stem is half as tall again as the foliage. The rhizomes have a sturdy central-growing tuft with thick stolon-like side rhizomes and heavy white roots attached. Struggling to exist, *I. susiana* is a miserable sight, but grown well, it is a lovely and exciting flower.

I. gatesii is a very large-flowered species from northern Iraq and northern Turkey. Brian Mathew comments that it is extremely variable in colour in the wild. He gives the overall impression of the colour as greyish, brownish or purplish, depending on the amount of fine veining and stippling on the segments. Jean Stevens says this largest of all the species has almost unbelievably delicate ruffled flowers of pale grey silk of incredibly fine texture. The delicacy of the effect is caused by the fine network of tiny soft purple dots on the grey-white ground. The difference between these two colour descriptions indicates considerable variation in the colour and pattern of markings, and, of course, some allowance must be made for the eye of the beholder. Under any circumstances it is a strange and beautiful flower. Both standards and falls are nearly 13–20 cm across in a well-grown flower. The styles are thickly spotted with purple and are arched and curved over the fall with its signal patch of soft purple. The beard surrounds the patch area with a rather diffuse band of hairs, which may be yellow-brownish or purple-brown.

I. lortetii is another of the dramatic species, so extremely beautiful and difficult to grow that it has been the despair of many gardeners who have been inspired by its beauty and thwarted by its temperament. It is a native of the Middle East, where it grows at a height of 700 m above sea-level. It is a fairy-tale flower with large waved pinkish lilac standards of silky gauze and opulently rounded convex falls, slightly deeper than the standards and exquisitely pin-dotted and dusted with crimson. Rounded lilac-pink style arms curve over a soft brown beard. It carries its single flower on a 30 cm high stalk.

REGELIA IRISES. This is a relatively small group of irises quite closely related to the Oncocyclus but with two flowers to a stem and a beard on both the standards and falls. The flowers are much smaller than those of the large Oncocyclus but larger than those of the small species of that group. They are much easier to grow successfully, though admittedly not exactly easy. Like the Oncocyclus, they must have quantities of lime, perfect drainage and a hot dry position in summer. If there is any risk of summer rain, it is probably better to lift them every year, thus ensuring a complete, long rest before replanting in mid-autumn. They do not make winter growth, which probably accounts for the fact that they are easier than the winter-growing Oncocyclus. Like them, the seed of Regelias has a large aril and is very slow and erratic in germination. Although perhaps not so romantically and intricately beautiful as the Oncocyclus, their flowers are very lovely with rich and exotic colours. They have a unique shape, with long narrow pointed petals that are alluring and graceful. There are many lovely hybrids in cultivation, though these are not easy to find.

I. hoogiana is a comparatively recent (1913) introduction from central Asia and is the only Regelia with self-coloured flowers. These are a lovely light blue with a delicately fine, frosty sheen and a gold beard. No marks or veining destroy the purity of colour right into the base of the haft. The form is beautiful, with upright, slightly waved standards and drooping falls which, though broad at the haft, curve down to a point at the extremity of the falls. There is a peculiar sculptured precision to the flower which, together with the clean colour, produces an effect of quality and rare dignity. The foliage is a dull smooth green but is taller and more vigorous than in other species. *I. hoogiana* is the easiest of all the Regelia species to grow.

I. korolkowii is the best-known and one of the finest of the Regelia irises. It is a native of central Asia and grows to 40–60 cm, with the leaves 5–10 cm wide and purple-tinged at the base. The thick rhizome is only slightly stoloniferous. The type has flowers with somewhat pointed, very upright standards that meet at the top and rather pointed pendant falls. The colour is a greenish ivory with reddish veins, both in standards and falls, and the beard, as in all Regelias, is linear. The form *I. k.* var. *concolor* has light purple flowers. A small dark red-purple signal patch on the fall and red-purple style arms give colour to the flower. It is a beautiful iris and worth going to some trouble to grow.

I. stolonifera, like *I. korolkowii*, is not too difficult to grow. It is a vigorous species so named because of its habit of producing long stolons from the rhizomes. The erect leaves are 5–15 mm in width and the flowering stems reach a height of 30–60 cm. There are two or three flowers from each set of spathes, each about 7–8 cm in diameter. Both standards and falls are a strange mixture of browns and purple, brownish at the margins with a metallic blue sheen toward the centre. In some forms the linear beard is also a metallic blue. It is a variable species in colour and size and there are some named forms. This species has been instrumental in transmitting the showy metallic blue beard in the Regelio-cyclus irises, hybrids between the Oncocyclus and Regelia groups.

Crested irises or Evansias

The name Evansias commemorates the man who first introduced *I. japonica* into cultivation in Great Britain in 1794, Thomas Evans. Without exception they are all very beautiful and range from some of the tallest to some of the smallest plants in the genus. The tall ones are extremely graceful, adding a light and airy appearance to any area of the garden where they are grown.

The feature that distinguishes this group from the bearded irises is the fine serrated or toothed crest on the haft of the fall, in the same position as the signal patch in the beardless irises or the beard in those of the bearded section. In some members of the group the crest is microscopic, a faint furry pubescence, as is found on some of the beardless irises such as Dutch or Spanish irises. On the other hand, the crest in *I. tectorum* and *I. milesii* is so pronounced that at a casual glance one might be misled into thinking it a beard.

It should be explained that the crest of the crested irises is not what is called the ridge or crest in a diagram of the parts of an iris flower. This term applies to the twin pointed terminal ends of the style arms of an iris flower, as well as the little jagged fringe that distinguishes the Evansia irises. All irises possess the pointed style arm crests but only the Evansias have the fringes on the haft of the falls.

All the Evansias have flat strap-shaped leaves, broad in proportion to their height in most species, though narrow in the case of *I. gracilipes*. They vary in shades of green

I. japonica forma *pallescens*

44

— soft light green in the smaller species, deepening in colour until in some of the taller species it is quite dark and polished in appearance.

I. cristata, *I. lacustris* and *I. tenuis* from North America and *I. gracilipes* from Japan are the babies of the family. It is indeed difficult to believe that they are related to the soaring *I. wattii* or even *I. japonica*. However, small though they may be, all of them are extremely beautiful and have all the characteristics of their taller brethren. They make tiny fans, carrying flat flowers almost at ground level. *I. gracilipes* presents to our fascinated eyes tiny sprays of flowers on stiff thread-like stems. To view them adequately one needs to go down on one's knees, which is indeed a proper position before them. For those whose knees are stiffening, a raised pocket in the rock garden, if possible, would solve the problem, but however you view them the wonder remains.

I. cristata is a delightful little plant, very suitable for a rock garden and forming large patches when doing well. The small branched rhizomes produce fans of leaves usually less than 15 cm long at flowering time, although they tend to elongate later, and they are 1–3 cm wide. The green spathes produce one or two flowers, each of which is about 3–4 cm in diameter. Some forms have been named, but the form commonly seen is a clear lilac-blue. In the centre of the falls is a white patch and along this and down the haft run three very crisped ridges, which have a variable amount of yellow or orange-brown on or around them. The erect standards are much narrower than the falls and are self-coloured. The flowers are almost stemless on the rhizomes and it is the perianth tube itself, some 4–6 cm long, that holds the flower well above soil level. There are several white forms as well as a pink and a very clear blue.

In its native habitat, in the Appalachian and Ozark Mountains in eastern North America, it grows in moist woods, in more or less neutral soil on the flat or on banks or ledges. In warmer climates, some light shade is an advantage. The clumps must be lifted and replanted from time to time with plenty of leaf-mould, as they spread outwards and die out in the centre. The safest way to divide or move it is to lift out a divot of soil and, without breaking it up, replant in the new position. Even if one wishes to move only one rhizome, this is the best method after it has been severed from the main rhizome. This method can be used at any time of the year, otherwise division should be undertaken either in early spring before growth commences or after flowering. In this case great care must be taken to avoid drying out, and the plant should be kept watered until the new growth is well advanced. Do not attempt to shift plants in summer or late autumn, when their chances of survival will be slim.

I. lacustris, the lakeside iris, is confined to the Great Lakes region of North America. It grows in moist sands, gravel and limestone crevices, usually in slightly shaded areas in the edge of cedar and fir woods. It closely resembles *I. cristata*, to which it is indeed related. As well as being generally smaller in all its parts, *I. lacustris* also has a much shorter perianth tube, usually about 2 cm or less. The almost sky-blue flowers have a golden crest and a white patch on the falls, similar to that of *I. cristata*. Generally speaking, the leaves of the non-flowering fans of *I. cristata* are 1–3 cm wide and those of *I. lacustris* usually less than 1 cm. *I. lacustris* does not appear to be as robust as *I. cristata* and needs very careful culture. Exposure to full sun at any time quickly dries out the small rhizomes, but as long as they are protected by plenty of leaf mould and the light shade of overhead trees, they grow well. Division or shifting of the clumps should be undertaken in the same way as for *I. cristata*. Both these species have been

I. cristata   *I. lacustris*

known to rebloom, which is a most desirable attribute.

I. tenuis was at first linked with the Californian irises, largely on the basis of its distribution in Oregon. In general appearance it looks like a tall *I. cristata* but produces branched flowering stems 30–35 cm in height and small pale blue flowers about 3–4 cm across. The crest is, in fact, a low undissected ridge, not a cockscomb-like structure as in the other species. It is a widely creeping plant with long thin leaves, about 30 cm long and 1–5 cm wide. It inhabits cool leafy soil in Douglas fir forests or in dense undergrowth.

I. gracilipes is a small graceful Japanese species from the mountains of Hokkaido, Honshu and Kyshu; it is found also in China. It grows on wooded slopes in soil rich in leaf-mould, and in New Zealand and Australia it should be grown where it will be protected from the heat of the summer sun. Grown in full sun, the leaves become almost yellow-green and the flowers are undersized; grown in the shade in leaf-mould or compost-enriched sand, the foliage is an attractive light green and the flowers much deeper in colour, larger and daintier. This fairy iris, which has been referred to as the daintiest of all irises, is so lovely that too much care can never be taken to grow it to perfection. It flowers in late spring and the flowers, which are carried on slender wiry stems about 10–15 cm tall, are 3–4 cm in diameter and are lilac-blue with a large white zone veined with violet in the centre of the falls. The crest is mostly white with yellow at the apex. There is an exquisite white form, with snowy, ethereal flowers, which is just as easy as its blue sister, provided always that the rules are obeyed: it must never dry out.

Propagation is by division of the clumps during the growing season or immediately after flowering. Great care must be taken to see that the newly set divisions do not dry out as the little rhizomes become brittle and wither very quickly if not moist enough. The roots are very fine and the clumps should not be divided into too small pieces but should be left with generous growth tufts. A good mulch of leaf-mould or damp sphagnum moss tucked around newly shifted plants protects the fine roots, keeps the plant moist and generally helps it to re-root in its new quarters. A watch needs to be kept also on established plants as the summer advances, as the tiny rhizomes have a habit of rearing themselves out of the ground, presumably seeking more comfortable living space. Keep plenty of leaf-mould above and around them so that they do not dry out, as they will quickly do in the summer heat.

I. confusa is a vigorous clump-forming plant producing short stolons and slender erect stems up to 1 m in height, resembling bamboo canes. There are fans of broad leaves at the apex of the canes and in early spring the widely branching flower stems arise from these fans. There is a long succession of short-lived flowers, about 4–5 cm across and flat, white with yellow and sometimes purple veining around the yellow crest and signal patch.

I. japonica is perhaps the best-known of the Evansia irises and has been grown for at least two centuries. It is a native of China and Japan, where it grows in woods and moist places. The plant has slender creeping green rhizomes and long strap-like leaves up to 10 cm wide and about 80 cm long, dark green above and lighter below. If grown in full sun, the leaves become a rather sickly yellowish green, so give it a semi-shaded situation with rich, well-drained, acid soil. It is a vigorous grower and rapid increaser, and has the wandering habits of the other species in the section. In climates where hard frosts do not check it, it will grow around the year. It is extremely shallow rooting and divisions can be pulled away from the parent clump by hand, and they will come away with a generous supply of fibrous roots intact. The main rhizomes send out sheathed shoots that emerge at a slant as light green spears from 16–18 cm away from the plant. The flowers are produced in late winter and early spring and are carried on much-branched sprays 40–80 cm in height. The sprays produce a continuous supply of delicate pale lavender flowers, 4–5 cm in diameter, for six weeks to two months. These flowers are daintily fringed and frilled and have a tiny white, orange-tipped crest with a few tiny purple dots surrounding it. When growing well, up to a dozen flowers may be out at the same time, although up to six is more common. In the centre of the flat blooms the style crests with long, finely feathered tips stand upright.

I. milesii is a much more upright plant than *I. japonica* and has attractive wide, heavily ribbed leaves of a bright light green colour. It is easily grown in most well-drained soils, which should be rich in organic matter, loose and friable; it does not like lime. A site in full sun gives the best results. A good healthy clump is most effective in the garden, more for the beauty of the foliage than for the showiness of the flowers. The flower stems rise upright to a height of 30–75 cm and are slender and many-branched. For such a broad and vigorous-leaved plant the flowers are surprisingly small. They are much frilled and the falls have a peculiar form, flat at the haft and for half of their spread and then reflexing downwards. The colour is light pinkish purple with deeper spotting. The crest is fine and almost hairy and is orange in colour. It has the virtue of remaining in flower over a long season and if picked lasts in the vase for a considerable time, as the faded flowers can be nipped off daily and will be replaced by a new crop. It dies down completely in winter, leaving bright green-ringed rhizomes on the surface of the soil.

I. tectorum, the roof iris, is so called because it was grown on the ridges of the thatched roofs of houses in some parts of Japan. It is a native of central and southwest China and appears to have been introduced to Japan from there many centuries ago. There are several explanations for the adoption by the Japanese of such an unusual practice. Possibly it was part of the thatch construction of the roofs, as a binding medium between the thatch and the wet clay which was used to complete the thatching. The explanation I prefer is much less practical but very human and romantic. The Japanese women used the roots to make face powder but in times of famine there was no land to spare for such frivolous purposes. Being practical women, they realised that their thatched roofs provided a growing medium, so up went the roof iris and the lack of face powder was averted.

I. tectorum is a splendid iris with a slender creeping rhizome and fans of thin-textured, ribbed leaves about 2–5 cm wide, shiny light green in colour, which droop over in their upper length in a manner characteristic of many of the crested irises. The flower stems are slightly branched, sometimes with two branches, usually about 25–35 cm tall, and carry two or three flowers from each set of spathes. The flowers are large, about 8–10 cm in diameter and flattish because the falls are only slightly deflexed and the standards are held outwards rather than straight. This flat appearance makes the flowers very suitable for sprays or corsages. The flowers are a lovely shade of blue-lavender, with very light mottling of deeper colour on the falls and a white, prominently toothed crest. The two lobes of the style arms are very ragged, and these together with the undulating margins of the falls and standards give the whole flower a delightful frilly appearance. There is a lovely pure white form with gold-tipped crests. This white form, like many other albinos, comes true from seed when self-fertilised.

I. tectorum may be successfully grown in most well-drained soils but a little attention to its special needs repays handsomely with larger, cleaner-coloured flowers. The soil should be rich in organic matter, loose and friable, with the site in full sun and well drained. The roots are very shallow and as the plant is a rapid increaser it soon uses up the supply of available plant food. To keep the vigour of the plant and the size and clear colour of the flowers, it should be divided and replanted every two or three years. Provided the original site was well prepared, *I. tectorum* may be replanted in the same site if it is well dug over and some extra sheep manure or compost added. If the site is a really good one an amount of organic manure, or compost forked lightly around the plant, will provide the necessary boost, but will also encourage it to spread wider than is convenient. Division may be carried out shortly after the plants have flowered in the spring, or following the autumn rains. Lime is not essential except in very acid soils, but plants tend to do better after a light top-dressing of lime in early winter. It is frost-hardy in most parts of New Zealand, although the young growth will not stand spring frosts.

A number of attractive hybrids have been raised from *I. tectorum*. This species has

I. wattii

Evansia hybrid

I. tectorum, white form

been successfully crossed with *I. pallida* (a bearded iris) to produce 'Paltec', an attractive little iris with the light green leaves of *I. tectorum*, lightly ribbed, and pretty soft lavender-blue flowers with little or no markings. It grows and flowers freely in much the same conditions as *I. tectorum*.

I. wattii is the tallest-growing of all the Evansias and one of the loveliest. The foliage is very similar to that of *I. japonica* but the habit of growth is quite distinct. During the growing season, prior to the spring in which it flowers, slender bamboo stems slowly develop below the luxuriant fans of rich green leaves. Early spring finds these growths well developed. Then with the first sign of spring, the flowering spray emerges from the tall leaf fan. For some weeks the blossom spray develops until it is some 2 m long and generously branched. Buds open and the exquisitely frilled, clear lavender blooms begin their long flowering season. The large flowers are 6–8 cm in diameter, the standards are held at an angle of 30 degrees and the falls reflex slightly. Each spray produces over fifty flowers during the next three months of continuous bloom, and since every fully grown fan produces a flowering spray, a clump in full flower is a breathtaking sight.

I. wattii is a rapid increaser but, unlike *I. japonica*, it does not spread into an untidy mess. The flowering stems need staking, not only to keep the clump in shape but also to prevent them bending over with the weight of the fans. Because it grows so tall the plant needs protection from wind, otherwise the flowers can be torn and the very decorative leaves shredded. Offsets may be taken at any time of the year, as it makes growth all year round. Offsets should be cut off along the small but very tough side rhizomes and they will lift out with the fibrous roots intact. Another method of propagation is to cut the thick noded stems into lengths and plant as cuttings; every cutting will strike easily and send up shoots from the base of the cutting below ground level. These bamboo-like stems are really rhizomes that have taken to the air. The true stem begins at the base of the leaf fan and carries the flowers in sprays.

I. wattii is not particularly fussy in its soil requirements and does quite well in an east-facing situation with morning sun only. Although not as hardy as some of the Evansias, it does not seem to be damaged by light frost.

A number of Evansia hybrids have been raised. 'Question Mark' is a strong-growing plant with a good flower spray with the parentage *I. wattii* x *I. darjeeling* or *I. wattii* x *I. confusa*. 'Askomil', 'Kilkivan', 'Honiana', 'Bourne Graceful' and 'Nobody's Child' are other hybrids that have been registered.

Beardless irises

Siberian irises

Included here are irises from two groups — the Sibirica and Chrysographes series — and the host of hybrids derived from them. The most popular hybrids are derived from *I. sibirica* and *I. sanguinea*, which together constitute the Sibirica series. The Sibiricas are more easily grown, more lime-tolerant, and put on a superior display, however a number of Chrysographes irises are worth a place in the garden.

The Siberian irises are characterised by the slender grass-like leaves growing from very close-set wiry rhizomes, which are buried under the thick tufts of growth. Most

50

of them set seed readily and are easily raised. The different species within each group cross very easily, and to guarantee pure seed where more than one species is growing in the garden, it is advisable to pull off the falls and hand-pollinate the flower.

The flowers of the different species vary in form but all are slender in outline, excluding the modern, rather flat tetraploids. Another characteristic is the little flanges that project near the bases of the falls. As well, they have a peculiar and obvious stigma, shaped like a triangular tongue. Most of the species have hollow stems, straight and thin, and these, together with the characteristic stigma, are peculiar to the group.

All Siberian irises are more or less water-loving plants. However, they do not like to have their roots actually in water and do best in a site that is reasonably well drained. They will grow well in a border if ample water is supplied in spring. They are sun-lovers, although in climates hotter than their native habitats they flower quite well when they get sun for only half a day. Grown in full shade, they do fairly well but offer few, if any, flowers. As with many irises that prefer ample summer moisture, once established they do not object to late summer and autumn droughts. By the time these droughts are experienced, the re-rooting following the early summer flowering has been completed and the plants have a sufficient root system to stand up to the semi-dormancy imposed by a drought.

They are all deciduous, dying down in late autumn. The dead foliage looks untidy

A clump of *I. sibirica*

51

and unsightly until the new growth begins to push up. The dead leaves can be cut off but care must be taken to leave enough to protect the plant from water-logged conditions through the winter and from frost damage.

All the Siberians love good rich soil but dislike lime, preferring a somewhat acid soil. They may be given liberal quantities of organic matter either as a mulch or incorporated in the soil. The hardiest species are *I. sibirica* and *I. sanguinea*. Those grouped in the Chrysographes section are fussier about their growing environment and require moist conditions, at least until established. If conditions suit them, Siberian irises will stay happily in one place unless they become too crowded. If they must be divided, do so in early autumn for preference. Keep the pieces reasonably large for quicker establishment and do not allow them to dry out.

They generally come into flower when the Tall Beardeds are coming to the end of their season, and continue well into summer. Repeat-blooming hybrids are also being developed, and these produce a second flush of flowers in late summer and early autumn. In addition, there are tetraploid hybrids with larger flowers, better colour and better substance.

If you would enjoy the effect of swarms of butterflies in your summer garden, plant *I. sibirica*. In addition to its beauty, it is one of the easiest and least demanding of all irises. Give it a position in the middle of the border in good composty soil, with no lime, where it can bask in the sun for part of the day. Sit back and watch it grow and when summer comes enjoy your butterflies.

The species itself is rarely grown today; there are so many hybrids available that interest in the type plant has evaporated. It has a small, light blue or blue-purple flower, somewhat variable in tone and usually veined on the falls. The standards are rigidly upright and the falls distinctly pendant. It usually has a small side branch near the top of the stem, which is nearly twice the height of the foliage; this droops after it attains about 30 cm, therefore appearing shorter than its actual length. The terminal head produces three to five flowers and the side branches another two.

I. sanguinea is somewhat similar to *I. sibirica* but has a much larger flower on a more dwarf plant. The colour of the flower is decidedly deeper purple with a reddish cast and with heavier white veining on the haft. One characteristic that definitely helps to distinguish it from other Siberian species is the vivid red spathes and leaf bases. The foliage is somewhat broader and more drooping. The flower stem, up to 60 cm, carries only two flowers to a stem and barely reaches above the foliage. It is probably this species and the Japanese form with tall flower stems that have been responsible for much of the initial progress in the deeper-coloured hybrids, particularly the red-purples and dark blues. *I. sanguinea* is a plant of mountain meadows, open wet plains and light deciduous woods, and enjoys the same garden conditions as *I. sibirica*.

I. chrysographes is perhaps the most beautiful species among the Siberian irises. Its specific name, which translates to 'writing in gold', is perfectly descriptive of the delicate gold markings on the smooth petals, which are deep red-purple or lusciously black. There is a lovely form, var. *rubella*, common in cultivation with flowers of a deep reddish plum colour. The plant has the typical hollow flower stem and greyish green drooping leaves. The flowers are also deliciously fragrant. *I. chrysographes* is a native of southern China and northeast Burma, where it is found in moist pastures and marshes. It is quite easy to grow and is a superb garden plant. If I could have only one Siberian

Siberian hybrid 'Castlegrace'

species in my garden, my choice would be *I. chrysographes*, probably the cultivar 'Kew Black'.

I. clarkei is distinguished from the other Siberian species by its solid stem. The forms I have seen have varied from china-blue to a slightly darker blue with a large white, violet-veined patch in the centre of the falls. It is widespread in the eastern Himalayas and occurs on hillsides in damp grassland and sometimes at the edge of rhododendron and *Abies* forests. In some areas it is said to be so plentiful that it is cut and dried for fodder for horses and yaks, although it is not grazed while it is green or in the growing state.

I. delavayi is one of the tallest species in the group, attaining 1.5 m in height, and also has the broadest foliage. It was introduced to Western gardens in the 1890s by the French missionary the Abbé de la Vaye, who found it growing in swamps in southwestern China. It seems to be even taller growing in the southern hemisphere

Siberian hybrids 'Anne Dasch' and 'Anniversary'

than in England, especially if grown beside water. It is a rapid increaser and takes over more than its share of garden space. The rhizomes are large and tough, and unless clumps are divided before they become too large, a very sharp spade or even an axe is necessary for division. It is easily raised from seed but needs to be hand-pollinated as, together with other Siberians, it is liable to hybridise with any of its near relations who happen to be handy. One of these hybrids — 'Delfor', a cross with *I. forrestii* — is sometimes available. *I. delavayi* will also hybridise with *I. clarkei*, *I. wilsonii* and *I. chrysographes*.

The provenance of *I. bulleyana* is rather doubtful and it seems highly probable that it is a hybrid between *I. forrestii* and *I. chrysographes*. The leaves are slender and drooping and the plant is not as robust as most other Siberians. The light lavender standards are short and held at an angle of about 45 degrees , while the slightly rounded falls are lavender with gold at the haft and white veining down the blade. It is quite easy to grow and divide and is not fussy as to soil.

I. forrestii was collected and introduced in 1908 from China, where it is a plant of alpine pastures. It is a slender species 35–40 cm in height, sometimes less in the wild. The narrow linear foliage is glossy on one side, grey-green on the other, and much shorter than the flower stems, which are unbranched with a terminal inflorescence of two flowers. The flowers have clear yellow standards with slightly deeper falls with brownish purple veining on the hafts; the standards are erect. It requires somewhat more care in its culture than other Siberian species and is easily lost if allowed to remain too dry during the late summer. It is easily raised from seed and will flower the second year after germination. Seedlings vary considerably in the size of bloom and width of petals, with some seedlings being deeper in colour and much showier than others.

I. wilsonii is the only other yellow-flowered Siberian and, like *I. forrestii*, comes from China; it was collected in western China by E. H. Wilson in 1907. It also is a plant of alpine pastures on streamsides and rocky hillsides. This species is a larger plant than *I. forrestii*, up to 75 cm in height, and both sides of the leaves are grey-

54

Siberian hybrids 'Ewen' and 'Foretell'

green. The leaves are about equal in length to the flower stem, which is unbranched and carries two fragrant flowers. These are about 6–8 cm in diameter, larger than *I. forrestii*, and are pale primrose, with the broad falls veined and dotted with purple-brown, especially in the centre and on the haft. The standards are held at an oblique angle. It also differs from *I. forrestii* in the fruiting stage by having elongated pedicels up to 10 cm long (not more than 7.5 cm in *I. forrestii*). Unfortunately, as with other yellow species, it crosses freely with other species and loses its identity unless great care is taken.

In recent years many of the Siberian species have been crossed with the Pacific Coast irises or Californians to make a new race which has been called Cal-Sibs.

Pacific Coast irises

These beautiful and delicately flowered irises, also known as Californian irises, are inhabitants of the Pacific Coast states of western North America. There are eleven species in this group, however they interbreed freely and so a host of hybrids now exist. The hybrids range in colour from white to lavender, violet, purple, yellow and bronze shades, all with delicately veined petals, and newer forms have broader, more ruffled petals than the species.

The Pacific Coast irises are distinguished from other beardless species by several characteristics. On the whole they are recognised by their tough rhizomes with wiry roots, usually slender leaves and mostly unbranched stems. They also have a different chromosome count.

They are, as a rule, fairly dwarf plants around 40 cm tall, producing one or two flowers per stem, although the stems of some species bear three or four flowers. The flowers are of typical iris form, although the blades of the falls tend to flare out horizontally. In the southern hemisphere they tend to be evergreen, but in their native habitat some of the higher-altitude species are deciduous. They are, ecologically, montane plants occurring in neutral or slightly acid, gritty, well-drained soils in lightly wooded areas, although *I. douglasiana* can often be found on open coastal headlands and in heavier soils.

Most species are extremely variable, especially in flower colour. Their identification is also complicated by the frequency of natural hybrids. In garden conditions they hybridise freely and often produce the most beautiful offspring. They flower in spring.

They can be grown successfully in well-drained, slightly acid soil in full sun or slightly dappled shade. They do well under deciduous trees, where the soil doesn't become overly wet in winter and they are shaded from the hot summer sun.

Great care must be taken with all the Pacific Coasters to divide clumps at the right time of the year. Younger plants can be safely divided and transplanted immediately after flowering, provided that they are not allowed to dry out before their plentiful supplies of fat white roots have established themselves in the ground. In older clumps the heavy mass of fine fibrous roots makes it difficult to dissect the plant and, lacking the same proportion of white roots as the younger plants, they find it much more difficult to re-establish themselves. It is advisable therefore to divide when new white roots are forming, usually in late autumn or early winter. Never attempt to divide or transplant them during periods of drought.

Seed is easily raised and should be sown in autumn. Seedlings can be transplanted into permanent positions about 20 cm apart as soon as they are about 5 cm high. They should flower the second year from seed and may be left undivided for three or four years at least. Well-worked soil greatly assists in bringing the seedlings into sizeable clumps. They should be given no organic manure nor lime.

I. douglasiana is the strongest-growing and coarsest-foliaged species in the group. The leaves vary from stiff and narrow to drooping and may be up to 2 cm wide. They are deep dullish green, stained red at the base. It is a true evergreen, even in cold districts, and very hardy, withstanding temperatures up to -10°C. *I. douglasiana* is a rapid grower and even seedlings make quite a sizeable clump in a year. At maturity (about two to three years old), a clump may be a metre across with leaves 20–70 cm long. Planted out as seedlings in the spring, they will flower the following year, producing five to seven stems the first year. It normally flowers from spring to early summer.

The flower stems usually overtop the leaves by several centimetres and often carry two or more side branches, making it unique in the group. The top spathe usually holds three flowers and the side branches two. The colour of the flowers ranges from a pale lilac or lavender to richer shades of lavender-blue to lilac with almost yellow hafts. Violet and purple forms were common at one time as well as an almost apricot pastel shade.

One of the distinctive features of this species is the D-shaped seeds, which are unlike those of all the other species in the group, except *I. innominata*. The seed pod is also more angular in shape.

Division of clumps is best carried out in early spring or autumn after the first rains but, except in cold climates with early winters, autumn planting is preferable. In wet climates they can be divided after flowering. Like many other irises, division of clumps can not be safely undertaken in drier districts. *I. douglasiana* is very easy to grow but prefers somewhat loose soil with a reasonable amount of humus or leaf-mould. In poor soils garden compost should be added but not lime.

I. fernaldii is a slender species about 20–45 cm in height with very grey-green

I. innominata

Pacific Coast hybrid

leaves about 7 cm wide with purple tinges at the base. The two flowers are atop a tube about 3–6 cm long, widened at the apex and sheathed by non-divergent bracts. The colour is a pale primrose-yellow with a deeper yellow median line on the falls and sometimes a faint purple tinge of veining. The style lobes are usually about 1.5 cm long and rather blunt at the apex.

I. hartwegii is a very variable plant and four subspecies are recognised. It is deciduous, about 10–30 cm in height, with narrow leaves and bracts that diverge and are separated from each other by up to 4 cm of stem. There is sometimes only one flower, but more often two, of a pale creamy yellow or lavender, often veined darker. They have a very short perianth tube that is often quite thick. The falls and standards are narrow so that the flower lacks substance. It is hardly a spectacular plant, although the shorter and more compact forms are dainty and attractive.

I. innominata is the loveliest species of them all and probably the best known and most sought after of the series. One of the most beautiful of spring-flowering plants, it has an exceptionally long flowering season, coming into bloom in early spring and slowly, over the next six weeks, increasing the number of stems in flower until every clump is a rainbow of colour. It is effective in a border or as a specimen plant in a rock garden. A group of seedling clumps will give a display for two to three months or longer in a mild climate.

The species occurs in a wide range of colours, from palest yellow through to apricot, bronze, shades of brown to dark red-brown, from pale lavender to deepest purple and shades in between. The form and shape of the falls are very varied, nevertheless *I. innominata* is not easily confused with the other species of the series. In the best forms the standards and falls have sufficient width to close the gap between the petals. The stem varies from 15 to 25 cm tall. The foliage is evergreen when established, but autumn divisions often lose most of their leaves during the first winter. The base of the leaves and stems varies from almost red to a flushed pink. Seedling plants may not show this colour in the early stages but mature plants invariably do.

Although the species is sometimes found in moist places, and in some gardens will tolerate such conditions, generally speaking *I. innominata* is very intolerant of poor drainage. On heavy soils the plants do not like a badly drained situation. Although the plant will flourish in the summer under such conditions, come winter, when growth slows down, it will suddenly turn brown and collapse. It grows quite well in part-shade but flowers more profusely in full sun.

This desirable species normally produces two flowers from the top spathe and one from a small side branch. Towards the end of the flowering season the later-formed stems often produce a second side branch; then the top spathes may produce three flowers and each branch two. Some seedlings are more inclined to this late-season branching than others. Improved forms produce many well-branched and many-flowered stems in every possible jewel shade. For floral decorations, posy-bowls, posies and shoulder sprays, the flowers are unequalled, so light, dainty and perky are they. There are also some lovely hybrids between *I. douglasiana* and *I. innominata*.

I. macrosiphon (syn. *I. amabilis*) is sometimes regarded as being synonymous with *I. chrysophylla*. As the name implies, the perianth tube of this species is large, although there is considerable variation in its length. As with *I. chrysophylla*, some forms are very compact and are almost stemless. The stem carries two flowers, which vary in

58

Hybrids of *I. innominata*

colour from white and cream through shades of yellow to deep gold, from pale lavender through to violet and deep purples. Hybridisation has resulted in the production of dark reds, red-browns and red-purples. Some of these are almost unveined, although generally there is a delicate tracery on the falls. Altogether the species is somewhat similar to *I. innominata*, although perhaps not so attractive in growth.

I. munzii, the blue-flash iris, is one of the largest flowered of the Pacific Coasters and one of the bluest among the rhizomatous irises. It is a robust plant, up to 75 cm in height, with grey-green leaves 1.5–2 cm wide. The bracts are divergent and separated by as much as 6–19 cm of clear stem. The two to four flowers have a thick tube 7–10 mm long. The colour is always in the blue-purple range, from pale blue or lavender to deep reddish purple. There is often a startling vivid blue streak or flash up the centre of the falls. Both falls and standards are often waved, sometimes frilly at the edges. It is a lovely flower but is rather frost-tender.

I. purdyi has a rather flat, almost squat-shaped flower with many short bract-like leaves all the way up the stem. These and the true leaves are dark green and strongly tinged pink or red at their bases. The two flowers are straw coloured with rigid standards held at an angle of 45 degrees, the falls having the usual red-brown veining of many of the Pacific Coasters.

I. tenax (syn. *I. gormanii*) was the first of the series to be brought into cultivation

Pacific Coast species *I. tenax*

I. longipetala, one of the Rocky Mountain species

60

and is one of the easiest to grow. Unfortunately, it is rare to see a clump of true *I. tenax* plants as it is one of the worst offenders for hybridising in gardens. It is a delightful little iris, making a neat clump with narrow leaves to 50 cm long, rather lax and longer than the flowering stems, which are produced in great profusion on mature plants and usually carry only one flower. The daintily poised flowers with upright standards vary, in a most intriguing way, in their pencilled markings. They range through all gradations of colour, through shades of bright rose and purple to palest lilac and deep heliotrope, all with primrose or yellow veinings. The flowers are comparatively large and held well above the foliage. A mature plant with its plenitude of stems makes an intense spot of colour in the garden.

I. tenuissima is a slender species, usually 15–30 cm tall with grey-green leaves 4–6 cm wide and bracts that are held erect round the tube. The two flowers have narrow horizontally spreading falls, giving them a rather starry appearance, although they are quite large with a long slender tube about 3–6 cm long, the upper quarter of which is expanded and nearly cylindrical. The colour is creamy with purple or brown veining on the falls. A distinctive feature of the species is the long, narrow, pointed style lobes, which are strongly reflexed.

Rocky Mountain irises

These are robust plants hailing from the Rocky Mountains of North America. Only two species are now recognised (some authorities regard even these as the same), which are not easily separated from some of the other series, although they seem to constitute a distinct unit if ecological, geographical and morphological characters are combined. They are confined to calcareous soils that are very wet in winter and spring and dry in summer. They have tough, wide-spreading, thick rhizomes clothed with old leaf remains. The fruiting stem persists for the best part of a year or more and carries six-ribbed capsules, tapered at both ends.

I. longipetala is a stocky plant with thick stems 30–60 cm in height. The dark green, rather glaucous basal leaves are usually just exceeded by the flower stem. As well there are two smaller stem leaves. The spathes contain three to eight flowers and one of the striking features of the plant is the large head-like inflorescence on an unbranched stem. The flowers are veined lilac-purple on a pale lavender or near-white ground. The standards are much less veined than the falls, which may have a slightly yellowish signal patch in the centre. True to its name, *I. longipetala* has long petals, the long falls being deflexed with an attractive floppy appearance. Cultivation of this attractive garden plant is easy, provided it has a good loose soil and perfect drainage. If it is well drained, a somewhat heavy soil suits it best. Again, no lime must be applied.

It is easily raised from seed, but takes two years from germination to flowering. Division is best undertaken immediately after flowering, as its early flowering allows the bloom season to be well over before the onset of summer dryness. Care should be taken not to break the roots when dividing as the root system is not as large as in the larger irises.

I. missouriensis (syn. *I. tolmeiana*) is similar in many respects to *I. longipetala* but is a much more variable plant, being extremely widespread in the wild. It is more slender and the leaves usually overtop the flowers which, as a rule, number two or three in each set of spathes. The flowers resemble those of *I. longipetala* but the ground colour ranges from pale blue or lilac to deeper shades. The falls are prominently veined, particularly toward the base, with a yellowish signal patch. It has a very wide distribution in western North America in meadows, along stream-banks, in scrub or pine forest, but always in areas that are wet until flowering time but dry thereafter. It flowers rather later than *I. longipetala*.

Water-loving irises

The Laevigatae series come from watersides, ditches and swampy grasslands in Europe, Asia and North America, and include such familiar irises as *I. pseudacorus* from Britain and Europe, the Japanese irises (*I. ensata*, syn. *I. kaempferi*, and *I. laevigata*). They are tall vigorous winter-dormant plants with stout rhizomes and rather wide leaves. Being water plants, they produce seeds that are capable of floating, and the capsules are thin-walled, breaking up irregularly or rotting away rather than splitting open to release their seeds, as is normal with most irises.

All the species do well in damp places in the garden or on the margins of ponds and streams where a plentiful supply of moisture can be maintained, especially in the summer. The soil needs to be acid and built up with water-retentive peat, leaf-mould, well-rotted manure or compost. If the soil is not acid enough, apply a light dressing of sulphur. They dislike lime. Some are happy to grow right in water. Apart from *I. pseudacorus*, they are rather difficult in a mixed border where other plants may not

I. ensata planted with other water-loving plants.

62

Two *I. ensata* hybrids

63

take kindly to all the water required by the irises during the spring and summer growing season. A bed can be made for them by digging out a good hole, lining it with plastic with holes pierced in it, then filling the hole with the soil mix. It should be slightly lower than the surrounding bed for ease of flooding.

I. ensata (syn. *I. kaempferi*) is widely grown, both in the wild form as well as many cultivars. The wild form grows about 60–90 cm in height and the flower stem overtops the foliage. The leaves have a very prominent midrib, which distinguishes it from *I. laevigata*, whose leaves are completely smooth. The flower stem is either unbranched or occasionally has one branch and carries three or four flowers, which in the wild form are a glowing reddish purple in the early morning sun. The falls have a yellowish haft, the yellow spreading to the base of the ovate blade. The standards are smaller and erect. They must have plenty of moisture during the growing season and be kept moist until late summer to enable full root development to occur. They require a winter rest and so will not tolerate winter waterlogging or permanently boggy situations. Divide plants immediately after flowering about every three years and plant the rhizomes about 7.5 cm deep. Hybrid varieties have large flat blooms 20–30 cm wide with overlapping petals and are often double or triple. Modern cultivars come in a range of colours from white to purples, blue and red-violet and often have intricate markings.

I. laevigata has lovely rich blue flowers with broad pendant falls with somewhat narrower upright standards; the falls have a central ridge of light yellow. The leaves are smooth, light green, rather thin and droop at their upper end. Forms of *laevigata* include 'Semperflorens' (blue), 'Regal' (plum-coloured), 'Alba' (white), 'Albopurpurea' (white with blue spots), 'Albopurpurea Colchesterensis' (blue with a white star). Together with *I. pseudacorus* it will tolerate bog conditions. When planted in water it will reach 2 m high with much larger flowers than those on plants grown in ordinary garden conditions. The stems are rounded and rarely straight. Two or three flowers are produced at the terminal spathe, and one or two side branches are usually produced. The height of the stem and the size of the flowers depend entirely on the richness and dampness of the soil. The rhizomes should be planted at least 2–3 cm below the soil surface. They are covered with the fibrous remains of the previous season's growth. The plant slowly spreads away from its original position and therefore should not be planted too close to other plants. Increase under good conditions is fast, but it quickly uses up the available humus, and the soil should be topped up every winter with a good dressing of well-rotted manure or rich compost. It dies down entirely in winter, coming back into growth in the middle of spring. When it is to be grown in a bog or water garden it should be transplanted after flowering in spring or early summer. In ordinary garden soil it is better to plant in early spring or early autumn, preferably the latter.

I. pseudacorus is the common yellow flag, the only yellow-flowered species in the series and quite distinct from any other water iris. It is a tall plant, up to 1.6 m in height, and has grey-green leaves. The four to twelve yellow flowers, the number depending on the dampness of the site, usually have some brown or purplish veining on the falls and a darker yellow zone. However, some forms lack this dark blotch, as in var. *bastardii*. The standards are quite short and narrow. *I. pseudacorus* flowers in early summer and will cover large areas alongside streams and ponds.

I. laevigata *I. laevigata* 'Alba'

There is a variegated form of *I. pseudacorus* that is a useful garden plant. It is not nearly so robust as the type and has indifferent and uninteresting pale flowers but, in a good plant, the clear, pale gold leaves with a light green edging are very attractive and merit a place in a partly shaded border that is moist and humusy. This variegation turns to green as summer progresses.

I. versicolor is a robust clump-forming American species, rather coarse in growth with heavily ribbed, very broad foliage. The creeping wiry rhizomes are very tough and when cut are pink. As well there is a purplish red base to the fans where they rise from the root. The branching stems carry several flowers in shades of violet, blue-purple, lavender or dull slaty purple in summer. The falls are widely spreading and often have a greenish yellow blotch at the centre of the ovate blade, surrounded by a white area variegated with purple veins, which continues down the fall. There is also a white form, but a particularly desirable form is 'Kermesina' with lovely rose-purple flowers. It is smaller in growth and a good garden plant. Seed of *I. versicolor* is freely produced and easily raised, and will flower the second year if well grown. Divide old clumps either in autumn or early spring, except in wet positions, when the best time is after flowering. It is entirely deciduous. Avoid applying lime to this species.

I. virginica is very similar to *I. versicolor* but not as easy to grow. It is commonly called the southern blue flag and has a bluer flower than *I. versicolor*. The height varies

I. pseudacorus   *I. pseudacorus* 'Variegata'

considerably, from 20 to 80 cm tall, and the stems are often arching and finally fall to the ground in the fruiting stage. The leaves are soft, yellowish green with drooping tips. The stem occasionally has one branch but is more often unbranched. The one to four flowers have spreading falls of blue, blue-violet, lilac, lavender or even occasionally pinkish lavender. In the centre of the oblong or obovate blade there is a prominent yellow hairy patch, which helps to distinguish this species. The standards are erect and smaller, narrowly obovate or spathulate in shape. An albino form is sometimes available. *I. virginica* flowers in early summer. It is a vigorous plant, easy to grow in good humusy soil, and comes freely from seed.

Louisiana irises

This group consists of five species of large-flowered water irises. The beautiful and popular Louisiana hybrids are large and robust plants with branched inflorescences, leaf-like bracts and large flowers up to 20 cm in diameter. They are useful cut flowers, with flowers continuing to open for up to 10 days.

All the species and natural hybrids are native to areas that are swamps in winter but dry out in summer and autumn. They do best in warm humid climates, but most will tolerate light frosts, and mulching in autumn will help protect them from more severe frosts. They do not like dryness in spring; drying out in summer is less crucial.

66

I. nelsonii,

However, growing well does not necessarily mean successful flowering. Whether in swampy conditions or in the garden, they should have an open aspect, and full sun is preferred except in hot districts where filtered shade is preferable. Being swamp-loving plants, they require a rich acid soil, preferably heavy. They should be well mulched in summer to protect the long surface-creeping rhizomes. A bed prepared as for the water-loving irises is ideal, with as much water as possible until flowering is over. Some forms, particularly those related to *I. hexagona* and those from Florida, may not be hardy in cold areas, where they will do best in a rich well-drained soil that does not dry out in summer. These irises are rather vigorous and have a habit of spreading over quite large areas although most of the modern hybrids are compact. If it is possible to dig a sunken patch for them, they will be somewhat checked.

The modern hybrids vary widely in form, size, height and colour; some are exquisitely beautiful. The colour range is wide, in every shade of blue, lavender, wine-reds, crimson, terra-cotta shades, yellow, creams and tangerines. Many are very tall and grow well over 1 m, especially in swampy places, but others are quite small, only 30 cm or so high. Division of plants, except in wet places, should be undertaken in early autumn every two or three years. In swampy or really wet soils, just after flowering is a suitable time. Plants can be moved all year round. The seeds are very large with a cork-like coat that enables them to float, the usual method of seed dispersal in waterside

Two Louisiana hybrids: 'Clara Goula' (above) and 'Just for Joe'

Louisiana hybrids 'Ann Chowning' (left) and 'Full Eclipse'

plants. Seed should be sown as soon as it is ripe and before the corky covering has had time to dry out. If the seed dries out so that the cases are hard, germination is very slow or may not occur at all. It usually takes two years for the seedlings to reach flowering size. Rust and leaf spot can affect Louisiana irises, particularly if they are grown without sufficient water.

I. brevicaulis (syn. *I. foliosa*) is a rather short plant for the group, attaining 30–50 cm in height. It has long slender rhizomes, and stems that zigzag at the nodes. The large stem leaves overtop the flowers and are quite wide, giving the plant a rather leafy appearance. There are several flowers produced terminally and, as well, from the axils of the leaves. These give rise to gorgeous bright blue-violet flowers up to 10 cm in diameter. The large, broadly ovate falls are reflexed and the much smaller standards are widely spreading rather than erect or drooping. In the centre of the falls is a yellow median band, and the hafts are usually veined whitish green.

I. fulva (syn. *I. cuprea*) is a robust plant, 45–80 cm in height, with slender green rhizomes producing straight or slightly zigzag stems with leaves that droop slightly at the tips. The flowers are smaller than those of the other species in the group, but are striking because of their red, coppery or orange-red colour with both falls and standards drooping, leaving the small style branches standing up at an oblique angle. It usually flowers in early summer and is an easy plant to grow but sometimes suffers from rust. Var. *lutea* is a pretty pale yellow form. *I.* x *fulvala* is a handsome red-purple hybrid

69

between *I. fulva* and *I. brevicaulis*.

I. giganticaerulea has very thick, light green, sword-like leaves that reach 70–180 cm long. The flowers are flat, up to 14 cm across, and are a lovely light blue. The tall stout stem zigzags slightly from the two short side branches. The long tough rhizomes spread quickly from the planting site and may be all of 45 cm away by the following growing season. It likes a rich soil and full sun. It is probably to this regal beauty that so many hybrids owe their size and height.

I. hexagona stands apart from the rest of the Louisianas as it occurs much further east than the other species and has not been used in the development of the great range of Louisiana hybrids, which are derived from the other four species. It has branching stems about 30–90 cm in height with strong stem leaves. The large flowers are a shade of blue-purple or lavender with a yellow signal patch in the centre of the falls. The haft is often speckled white or yellowish, shading to green on the lower part. The standards are upright and much narrower and more pointed than the deflexed falls.

I. nelsonii has stems 70–110 cm tall bearing several short stem leaves and usually a few branches. The basal leaves are 1–3 cm wide, frequently with drooping tips, and are a pale green. As in *I. fulva*, the large flowers, up to 10 cm in diameter, have reflexed falls and standards. The colour is reddish purple. Before their description as *I. nelsonii*, the populations of these reddish-flowered irises were known as Abbeville Reds, since they are restricted to the Abbeville swamp in central-south Louisiana. Modern hybrids number in the hundreds. They have a greater colour range than that of the Tall Beardeds as a result of the influence of *I. nelsonii* blood. These are best acquired from a specialist nursery.

Spuria irises

The Spurias are one of the tallest members of the genus. As handsome back-of-the-border plants, the larger species of the group, such as *I. orientalis* and *I. monnieri*, are unsurpassed. They may reach 1.8 m in height, with stiff sword-like leaves of a fresh green, and the flowers are variously coloured. At the other end of the scale are several small species better suited to the rock garden or front of the border, for example, *I. graminea*, *I. sintenisii* and *I. kerneriana*. Apart from their undoubted garden value, the large Spuria irises are invaluable for use in floral arrangements. The colours of the flowers blend well with other material and the tall strong stems add depth and solidity to an arrangement. The small *I. graminea*, if you have enough to pick, makes a charming, sweetly scented small pot.

Hybridisers, particularly in the United States, have worked steadily over the years with the tall species to produce beautiful colour combinations in the flowers and stately dignified stalks. The colours are always clear — frosty white, blues in many shades, creamy yellows through to almost orange, intriguing dark shades of tan, brown and almost black, in plain colours and varying combinations. Rising on stiff strong stalks amid the clump of solid sword-like leaves, these flowers hover like bright butterflies in a mixed border. A bed devoted to them alone is a glorious sight during the season, but unless the garden is large, so much space could hardly be spared for plants that are out of bloom for eleven months of the year. However, if it can be done, the massed effect for the flowering month is well worth it.

The tall Spuria 'Caramel Creme' is ideal in a
large garden.

A mass planting of the Spuria *I. orientalis*

71

The Spuria group is very distinct. The cylindrical seeds are encased in a paper-like bag, and the sharp-pointed seed pod has two hard ridges running down the full length of each of the three sections. They have fibrous rhizomes that grow on from the same point each year, and most species spread well beyond the original position in which they were planted. The larger species are slow to increase, as only a few side growths are made from each rhizome. When the old leaves of the summer growth die away in the autumn, the growing points of the rhizomes extend under the ground as fat growth buds extending beyond the point from which the previous year's leaves arose. The new leaves sometimes appear before the old ones are properly dried off, but until this new growth appears, either in winter or early spring, this growing point remains a clean hard pointed knob. The rhizome itself is stringy and fibrous, ringed with darker bands, and does not produce any further leaves. It is very tough and the dry wiry roots can be very uncomfortable to handle, being rather prickly. The new leaves appear as spears from the knob-like growing points.

The flowers closely resemble the Xiphium irises in shape, although they are more compact and inclined to hug the stems. Like Xiphiums, they are excellent for cutting. The leaves, except for the smaller species, are elegantly sword-shaped and upright, and very tough. This enables them to stand up well to rough weather. The flower stems are also strong and wind-resistant.

Taller Spurias and their hybrid descendants rejoice in plenty of sun, but their roots

Spuria hybrid 'Marilyn Holloway'

should be shaded. They like well-drained heavy loam, slightly on the acid side and require plenty of water during the growing season but like to be kept rather dry over summer. They respond to well-rotted manure and compost worked into the bed. In spring give them a dressing of a balanced fertiliser and in autumn a good mulch of compost. They do not like lime, although *I. kerneriana* and *I sintenisii* are fairly tolerant of soils with a high calcium content. They are such splendid background plants and flower so well when happy that it pays to cosset them.

Plants should be divided either in early spring in the case of the smaller species or in autumn in the case of the tall ones. They can all be shifted after flowering, but they must subsequently be kept well watered until they are established. Spurias dislike being moved. If this is necessary, do so in autumn and keep them well watered.

The smaller species are good rock-garden subjects if conditions suit them. They react badly to summer and autumn droughts and need plenty of good humus-rich soil, which must not be allowed to dry out but which must be well drained. In warmer climates semi-shade is recommended.

I. crocea (syn. *I. aurea*) is a fine, vigorous plant up to 1.5 m in height with sword-shaped leaves up to 75 cm long. The inflorescence consists of a terminal group of flowers and sometimes up to three branches, which are erect and stay close to the stem. The rich gold flowers are 12–18 cm in diameter. The falls have wavy margins with the haft shorter than the blade. The standards are erect and also somewhat crinkled

Spuria hybrid 'Imperial Ruby'

73

I. graminea is one of the smaller Spuria species.

at the edges. This iris is a beautiful and stately garden plant, easily grown in a sunny border.

I. graminea is one of the smaller members of the group. This rather leafy plant is an attractive and useful garden iris with its deliciously fruit-scented small flowers. It grows in semi-shade and makes an excellent weed-suppressant when growing well. It makes no winter growth, although in warmer conditions the tiny green shoots will make an appearance in early winter but remain at ground level until spring. With the coming of spring the plant grows rapidly and soon develops a clump of finely ribbed, narrow, dark green leaves. This foliage frequently overtops the flowers nestling among the leaves with a leaf close against the flower spathe. The standards are deep lilac, the style arm is a rich magenta-purple, and the falls are veined with violet on a white ground and violet at the top of the blade. The prominent winged haft is often greenish or brown tinted, as is the lower part of each style branch.

I. kerneriana is a delightful slender species and is one of the most attractive of the small Spurias for the rock garden or front of the mixed border. It grows up to 30 cm in height with dull green, linear foliage that is rather sparse in comparison with *I. graminea* or *I. sintenisii*. It is quite upright, very slender and lightly spiralled. The flower stems overtop the foliage by several centimetres. The rather inflated bracts enclose two to four flowers, each about 7–10 cm in diameter. They have arched recurved falls, the blade curling right over so that the tip sometimes almost touches the stem. The style arms also branch over, following the curve of the falls, but the standards remain erect.

The basic colour of the flower is a soft lemon-yellow or deep cream with a deep yellow blotch in the centre of the blade of the falls, fading towards the margins. The individual flowers are not long-lived and wilt rapidly but remain attached to the stem, which rather detracts from the appearance as the later flowers come out. The elliptical blade of the falls, 1.5–2 cm wide, narrows abruptly to the 5 mm haft. It has tubby seed capsules with a narrow beak up to 1 cm long. The foliage dies down completely towards the end of autumn and disappears in a few weeks. The site needs to be carefully marked, as when it is completely dormant in winter there is no indication of it above ground at all. Growth appears rather late in the spring, but once it does, it grows rapidly and the flowers open in early summer. It may be lifted and replanted, either in spring as growth starts or immediately after flowering. Plants shifted at this later stage must not be allowed to dry out until the new growth has begun. Under no circumstances should autumn or winter transplanting be undertaken. It is easily raised from seed, although this is sometimes slow to germinate, taking up to eighteen months or longer in the open garden. It is not fussy about the soil pH. It will not tolerate water-logged conditions, although it needs plenty of moisture in the spring, so good drainage is a necessity.

I. x *monnieri* is an attractive plant whose origins are somewhat confused, but it does appear to be a natural hybrid. It has the same stature as *I. orientalis* but the flowers

I. orientalis

75

are soft lemon-yellow in colour, somewhat less stiff than *I. orientalis* and with slightly broader petals. The foliage, too, is slightly broader and greener. Its new growth is well advanced by early winter and it greatly resents disturbance after the middle of autumn, taking several years to recover and re-establish itself if divided after the early growth is more than a few centimetres high — a generally sulky customer.

I. orientalis (syn. *I. ochroleuca*) is probably the best-known and most widely grown Spuria. It is a handsome plant, and an established clump adds character and distinction at the back of a border. The flower stems reach up to more than 1.5 m in height, more in damper situations. The somewhat sparse foliage, an interesting shade of greyish green, is a little shorter than the flower stalk. The large white flowers resemble a somewhat stiff Spanish iris and have a clear gold signal patch. There are two or three flowers in the terminal head, but several short side branches are produced which carry two flowers closely pressed against the stem.

I. sintenisii is another miniature Spuria, more dwarf and compact in growth than *I. graminea*. It produces low close tufts of growth, quite unlike the rather grassy clumps of *I. graminea*. Another difference is that it is evergreen, unlike *I. graminea*. It is free-flowering in spring, with a profusion of pretty blue-purple flowers with white veining on the tiny falls, on stems up to 30 cm in height. The rather solid linear leaves overtop the flowers as a rule. It is well worth a place in the front of a border or in a rock garden. *I. sintenisii* is not an easy iris to transplant and care must be taken to avoid damaging the roots when dividing a clump. The safest times to transplant are in early spring or after the first rains of autumn. It seems to prefer a somewhat heavy soil that is rich in calcium. Beware of letting it dry out before it is well established. Once established it will endure long summer and autumn droughts. It needs little or no manure but should be kept well supplied with good compost.

I. spuria itself has many named subspecies with little to distinguish them apart except, perhaps, habitat. There is considerable confusion among botanists and whether they should be regarded as separate species or merely subspecies seems debatable.

I. s. subsp. *maritima* (syn. *I. maritima*) is one of the commonest forms in cultivation. This iris is widespread in southwestern Europe and is the most western variant of *I. spuria*. It has the typical form with lateral buds hugging the stem. The straight foliage is somewhat glaucous and the upper stem leaves are longer than the stem internodes and help to conceal them. This characteristic helps to distinguish it from the typical form (*I. s.* subsp. *spuria*). The rather small flowers are blue-purple with a greenish yellow median stripe on the haft, which is longer than the blade.

I. s. subsp. *halophila* (syn. *I. halophila*) is one of the more easily recognised variants, since the flowers are primarily yellow and variously veined with pale blue, lavender-blue, or sometimes white flushed with gold. The blooms are smooth with good substance and they have an unusual outline, with very narrow segments elongated in proportion to the small square-bladed falls. This form occurs further east than *I. s.* subsp. *maritima* in eastern Europe, western Siberia, and the northern Caucasus and it inhabits wet meadows, often on riverbanks and frequently in saline soils. It is the most northerly growing Spuria in Russia, which is an indication of its extreme hardiness.

The species and the American-raised hybrids are superb garden plants either at the back of a border or in separate beds. Give them a good composty soil and some sun and they will settle down and require little attention for several years.

Other beardless irises

I. foetidissima is known as the Gladdon or Gladwyn iris as well as the stinking iris, on account of the horrible smell of the bruised leaves. It is the only member of its series. It is a variable plant, usually about 50 cm in height, with dark green tufts of evergreen leaves produced from compact tough rhizomes that spread rapidly. The rather flattened flower stem has two or three branches, each carrying one to three flowers, which open in succession. These flowers are a dirty grey-blue with a dash of dull yellow. Some forms are better than others, with more or less purple veining and whitish centres. There are also yellow variants of mild interest, some clearer in colour than others. When the seed capsule splits to reveal the scarlet seeds, the plant takes on a new aspect. These seeds hang on for several months and give a bright glow to a shady corner. They are useful in floral decorations, although the rather lax stems do not always hold the seed head erect. There is also a white-seeded form now available. The flowering period is early to mid-summer and the plant is quite useful for clothing shady untidy corners, where it acts as a successful weed suppressant. In some places this species is gazetted as a noxious weed.

I. lactea is a very variable and widely distributed species from central and eastern Asia. It presents no problems in cultivation, provided it is given an open situation and really well-drained soil. It survives long periods of drought and flowers quite freely, and is an attractive though not showy garden plant. It forms clumps with tough narrow

I. foetidissima   *I. lactea*

77

I. unguicularis 'Alba'   Seedling of *I. unguicularis* 'Starkers Pink'

leathery leaves of a peculiar dullish green; the leaves do not die down until late winter and are known to be salt-resistant. The resistance of the plant to a harsh environment is due partly to the tough deep roots, which enable it to survive in conditions where shallow-rooted plants would succumb. Each stem carries two or three fragrant flowers of a bright blue-purple in good forms, but rather dingy grey-blue in others. The flower shape is fairly distinctive because the falls do not spread widely but form a narrow V-shape. The colour is primarily blue, bluish purple or violet, the falls usually having a pale yellowish or whitish, dark-veined haft. The perianth tube is very short, 2–3 mm long, and the segments are all rather long and narrow, giving the flower a fragile appearance with little substance. Both falls and standards taper at both ends, the standards being narrower and shorter than the falls.

I. unguicularis (syn. *I. stylosa*) is the most desirable member of the entire genus. It begins to flower after the first shower in autumn and continues through the winter, tapering off in mid-spring. It needs as much sun as possible but will flower, if not so prolifically, in some shade. Well-drained soil, not too rich, suits it best and an occasional dressing of lime is acceptable. Plant out in spring and keep the soil moist until new growth appears. When dividing, make sure the clumps comprise at least several fans as they take some time to re-establish themselves. Indeed, this species doesn't require regular division to remain productive. As the flower has virtually no stem, just a long perianth tube up to 20 cm high, the seed pods sit at ground level and the seeds will

I. setosa

A waterside planting of *I. setosa*

germinate there if not removed. Seedlings will flower in their second year. Its worst enemies are slugs and snails, which revel in this delicate winter feast. Slug bait needs to be frequently applied, and at the beginning of winter it is beneficial to cut the leaves back by at least one third; this ensures there are no untidy old and long leaves to damage the delicate buds as they emerge, and also allows an uninterrupted look at the display of flowers.

The standards are narrow at the haft, which is reddish purple with fine brownish dots, but have wide broadly rounded blades. The falls are slightly deeper in colour with a narrow gold signal patch surrounded by a white area with conspicuous lavender-blue veins. The scented flowers come in blues of every shade from very pale to deep sky-blue, white and lilac-pink; there are also some vivid bluish violet forms, among them 'Mary Barnard' and 'Speciosa'. 'Alba' (white) and 'Walter Butt' (lavender-pink) are the first to flower in autumn. Another common form is 'Starkers Pink', a lilac-pink, which blooms later than *I. unguicularis* and is a smaller, finer-leaved variety. The species is also variable in terms of its growth habit and size. The largest and most vigorous forms are also much more free-flowering and more adaptable. *I. unguicularis* often becomes infected by virus, but seedlings will be virus-free.

A small relative from Crete is *I. cretensis* (syn. *I. unguicularis* subsp. *cretensis*). It forms grassy clumps and has very thin, glaucous foliage, usually about 25 cm long, extremely hard and wiry. The flowers are thin petalled and very dainty, produced to a height of 10–12.5 cm throughout winter. Unlike *I. unguicularis* in all its forms, the flowers of *I. cretensis* have little scent. The colour is an even, light violet in the standards, with red-purple hafts, and white-veined, lavender-violet in the falls. The flower has all the appeal of the true miniature. It is not too easily established, resenting any interference, and takes a year or two after planting before it flowers. It does best in a gritty, light, well-drained soil in full sun.

I. lazica resembles *I. unguicularis*, but whereas the species is a plant of hot dry climates, *I. lazica* is adapted to the humid subtropics and damper habitats. The foliage of *I. unguicularis* is held erect, but that of *I. lazica* is much longer and heavier and forms a wide leaning fan. *I. lazica* does better in cooler spots and it can tolerate considerably more shade. In mild climates it flowers in winter, but in a colder winter it will bloom in early spring. The flowers are large, vary from blue-purple to lavender, and are without scent.

I. minutoaurea, *I. verna* and *I. ruthenica* are three little irises that are a delightful addition to the garden, if you can obtain them. *I. minutoaurea* is a lovely miniature growing to 10 cm high whose very small flowers have pale yellow falls and primrose standards. The falls have a fine brown median stripe and the whole flower is slightly flattish. A sunny situation in the rock garden with loose friable soil suits it best. In colder areas the grassy foliage dies down in winter. Where it is warmer, it remains until the new foliage pushes it off. Slugs love it!

I. verna is a rhizomatous species that stands quite apart from other irises. Instead of a beard it has a gold pubescence of fine hairs on the lavender-blue falls, which have an intense gold median stripe. Lime is death to it, so it needs a cool acid root run with good winter drainage but plenty of moisture in summer. As it is a woodland plant, part shade is required. It forms quite a compact clump, but sometimes the rhizomes wander further afield to produce the small fans of greyish or deep green leaves. The flowers have a delicious scent and are borne singly on 5 cm stems.

I. ruthenica is a tufted iris with a short creeping rhizome and erect grassy leaves. The fragrant flowers are usually solitary on short stems. The falls are white with blue-lavender or violet margins; the standards and styles are wholly violet or bluish lavender. The standards and styles are held well up, nearly vertical, and are rather prominent. It is suitable for a rock garden in a sunny or semi-shaded, moist or dry position. Various Siberian species or even dwarf *I. setosa* are frequently offered for sale as *I. ruthenica*—it is a case of buyer beware!

I. setosa is an unusual iris in which the standards are reduced, often to bristle-like proportions, which gives the flower the appearance of having only three petals. It is a very variable species and has one of the widest distributions in the genus, ranging from eastern Asia through Japan across to Alaska, and in Labrador and the northeastern United States. *I. setosa* is easy to grow and an attractive garden plant. It prefers fairly moist conditions but does well in borders. The tall forms will flourish in any good garden soil if well supplied with water and the soil is free of lime. The smaller variants make delightful rock-garden plants.

It is very variable with several distinct forms. It varies greatly both in the depth of the blue or purple colour of the flowers and in the height of the stem. The Japanese forms are taller and more robust than those from Siberia, Alaska and Canada and have large purple flowers. The height varies between 15 and 90 cm from stoutish rhizomes, which are often clothed with the fibrous remains of old leaf bases. The leaves are often reddish tinged at the base and also vary in height. The stem is usually much-branched, although in the very dwarf forms it may be simple, with green bracts that are often purple edged. Normally the bracts enclose two or three flowers. The colour varies considerably, but in the Asiatic and northwest American forms it is usually purple-blue, whereas those from the eastern United States often tend to be a clearer blue. The narrow haft of the falls is veined purple and blue on a pale, yellowish or whitish background, and it expands abruptly into the broad orbicular falls. Both the standards and style arms are comparatively short and insignificant. Wet meadows, peaty bogs, light woods and shore lines are its natural home.

I. tridentata (syn. *I. tripetala*) has one or two delicately scented flowers with falls that are violet or blue-purple with darker veining and a whitish signal area, blotched yellow in the centre; the falls have the nearly orbicular shape of the species. It requires similar conditions to *I. setosa* and will grow in or out of water, preferably in light shade.

Bulbous irises

Xiphium irises

The irises of this group, which includes the Spanish, Dutch and English irises, are probably the best-known flowers in the whole genus. The Dutch irises have a wide market as cut flowers and are extremely popular garden plants. The foliage of most species appears in autumn, however *I. boissieri* and *I. latifolia* are exceptions, coming into growth in spring. In bulbous irises buds for the following season are formed during the last month or two of growth, and no amount of baking or drying out in summer, or the most careful culture, can produce blooms if no buds were formed the previous year. So to produce flowering bulbs, particular attention must be paid to culture in spring. Without doubt, a soil really rich in humus is a necessity, combined with good drainage. A hot sunny position and loose soil are equally necessary, as well as protection from frost.

I. xiphium, the Spanish iris, is the type species that gives the group its name. In the wild, the plant has several colour forms — two-toned blues, yellows, and combinations of whites, yellows and blues. All the forms have a yellow or gold signal stripe or patch below the crest, which is sometimes very velvety and prominent. One or two flowers are produced on wiry stems 40–60 cm tall. Our present-day Spanish irises are advanced-generation seedlings of these wild forms. Bulbs are normally sold as mixed colours, but named cultivars are sometimes available. They need a well-drained, sunny situation and protection from late frosts.

Early this century Dutch growers were successful in extending the flowering season of the Spanish iris by crossing it with other Xiphium species. One of the main parents of these hybrids was an early-flowering form (*I. xiphium* 'Praecox') with large flowers, blue falls and purplish blue standards. Another species used was the temperamental *I. tingitana*. The result was the new hybrid race of Dutch irises, which produce much larger flowers than the true Spanish irises and they also flower several weeks earlier.

Dutch irises are beautiful planted in groups. They make an exciting introduction to the new iris year, flowering as they do in the spring before the Tall Beardeds in early summer, but in many districts overlapping with the later-flowering Spanish irises. To grow them successfully, they should be given a reasonably rich, well-cultivated soil with some lime. Poor soil produces small flowers, but over-rich soil increases susceptibility to diseases such as black fungus, which attacks the bulbs, or viruses,

Opposite: Dutch irises

83

which cause blotches and markings on the flowers as well as unsightly yellowing of the foliage. The foliage should be rush-like and glaucous in the young stage. In maturity it opens out from the base into fairly broad, deeply channelled leaves. When cutting the flowers avoid cutting the stems too low down as this removes the valuable feeding leaves that help to produce the bulbs for the following year.

The bulbs can be lifted every year and divided, however the best flowers seem to come from bulbs that have not been disturbed the previous year, provided they are not crowded or have not worked themselves too near to the soil surface. They should be lifted when the foliage is dying down and dried carefully in a shady position under trees or in a dry airy shed. Late summer is a good time for replanting the bulbs, which should be planted about 8 cm deep with a little sand around them. Bulbs planted later than this start the season unprepared, without a good root system and in an essentially weakened condition; they are also more liable to disease and do not produce top-quality flowers.

I. tingitana, the Algerian member of the Xiphium group, is a provocative and elusive beauty that has been used in the development of some of the Dutch irises we grow. The blue 'Wedgwood' has *I. tingitana* in its ancestry and as a result blooms much earlier than some of the newer hybrids. It is a tricky subject and may flower as early as late autumn in warm sheltered spots, hence it needs a warm protected situation. It is very erratic in its flowering and many methods have been tried to secure regular blooms — leaving them in the sun or on an iron roof; baking them in the oven; and storing them in dry sand over summer. But none of these necessarily works. *I. tingitana* flowers when the spirit moves it, not when the gardener wishes. Throw them over the fence in exasperation and they will probably flower splendidly!

The blooms very much resemble a large Spanish iris, but the long lavender-blue upright standards taper to points; the falls are large and distinctly pendant, very blue on the waved margins, but much paler on the blade, which has a large golden signal patch of great substance. Well grown, it reaches over 1 m in height, with very broad glaucous foliage, heavily channelled and silvery on the upper surface. Two flowers open in succession from a terminal spathe.

Like all members of the Xiphium group, *I. tingitana* appreciates lime, which can be applied liberally. During the growing season, in winter and in spring, a top-dressing of potash should give an extra boost. The bulbs should not be planted too deeply — about 5 cm of soil above the tops of the bulbs is recommended — with sufficient space between each bulb to allow maximum development of the foliage. It is an advantage to place sharp sand above and below each bulb. Where there is a likelihood of occasional heavy summer rain, the bulbs should be lifted and stored in a dry place and replanted in autumn. The bulbs should not be lifted until the foliage has died down. Flowering-sized bulbs are very large, similar in size to a large-sized daffodil, with a well-rounded central bulb.

The foliage is hardy, but the flower buds are vulnerable to frost damage, particularly when in a forward stage of development. Buds will not stand frosts of over 5 or 6 degrees without injury.

This is a lovely iris, quite unbelievable when it opens its glorious blue flowers in mid-winter, and the silvery aluminium-coloured foliage makes a bright accent in the winter garden, even if no flowers appear.

The Dutch iris 'Wedgwood'

I. tingitana, an important species in the development of Dutch irises

Dutch irises

86

Dutch iris

I. juncea is perhaps the brightest member of the Xiphium group. Its vivid orange-yellow flower makes it a desirable bulb in any garden. The foliage is rounded, rush-like, somewhat straggly and a dull glaucous green colour. The flower itself is rather delicate, the falls being rather thin in substance, broad in the blade and finishing in a point. The second flower has a curious habit of rising on a long pedicel tube to a position slightly above that of the first flower. As well, the flowers have a pleasant scent. It is an altogether slenderer plant than the Dutch hybrids and grows around 30 cm high. *I. juncea* has an interesting bulb, quite different from any other bulbous iris. It has a peculiarly hard, dark brown skin, splitting into long fibres at its neck in stiff points. It grows reasonably well if its situation pleases it — a warm sunny position with plenty of sand, and lime, if the soil is heavy. Bad drainage is fatal, so place a layer of sand beneath the bulb at planting time. If the bulbs are doing well, they need lifting only every second year, otherwise lift them every year, but be careful to replant them before autumn. It is easily raised from seed sown in a sandy soil in a place relatively free from frost. The bulbs reach flowering size in the third or fourth year. It flowers at the same time as the Tall Beardeds.

I. filifolia is not often seen in cultivation. Its foliage is lax and almost rush-like and varies from thread-like to much broader in some plants. The plant can be easily identified by the curiously mottled sheath, which protects the young growth as it emerges through the soil. There are two distinct colour forms: one with lovely rich purple flowers with a blue, orange-margined signal patch and another with reddish purple standards with bright red-purple style arms and blue-purple falls. Two flowers are borne on stems 30 cm tall.

I. latifolia (syn. *I. xiphioides*) is the mis-named English iris, which, in fact, comes from the damp alpine valleys of the Pyrenees. It is the latest-flowering member of the Xiphium group, blooming in early summer and coinciding with the Japanese irises. Its cultural requirements contrast with those of the other Xiphiums. It will grow well in rich open soil that does not dry out in summer, but which, in winter, is never water-logged. It will grow in rather heavy soils but will not tolerate stagnant conditions. It also tolerates more shade than the other species and hybrids.

The leaves do not appear until rather late in the spring; they are fully mature by mid-summer and a month after flowering, the foliage dies away. Its foliage is quite distinct from that of its relatives. When half-grown, the leaves are very stiff, coming up in firm outward curves of broad channelled leaves, deep green on the outside, but silvery within. They have the leek-like appearance of the Junos. The two or three flowers are borne on heavy 30 cm stems. The spreading standards are short and very rounded and the falls, from a narrow funnelled haft, widen to almost circular, large ruffled blades. The whole effect is somewhat heavy. The colours range from shades of light to dark blue, lavender, violet, blue- and red-purples, to pure white. There are no yellow or bicoloured forms. Any marking or mottling of the pure and even colours is the result of a virus.

Seed is easily raised, but it takes four to five years for the bulbs to reach flowering size. It is better to let the young plants remain undisturbed for at least three years. They should be lifted when the foliage dies down and replanted immediately. This is essential, as in suitable conditions the bulbs begin to re-root within a fortnight of the leaves dying down.

Juno irises

These irises are an intriguing and very different group of species from the Mediterranean area and Central Asia. It is one of the largest groups within the genus, comprising over 50 species, but few are widely cultivated. They are not easy to grow, particularly in humid areas, as they are native to warm arid climates. Nevertheless, they are delightful, exciting and unusual plants and it is worth growing them if only for a short year or two. They are not always readily available because they are so temperamental and resent disturbance.

The Junos have thick-necked bulbs with thin brown tunics. Attached to the bulbs are thick white fleshy roots somewhat like radishes, which fork out from bulbs to a surprising depth in the soil. These roots are replaced each year, with new ones appearing at flowering time and the old ones shrivelling away, so that an undamaged bulb in its dormant state will have both new and old sets visible. The bulbs need careful handling, as these new storage roots are extremely brittle and can easily become detached from the bulb.

They flower in spring and die back in early summer. It is important they are then kept dry until autumn. They are perfectly frost-hardy. A topdressing of lime and blood and bone can be applied in autumn, but as they are not heavy feeders this is not crucial.

The shiny bright green foliage is distinct from all other irises. It is channelled in

The Juno *I. bucharica*

one plane so that the plants in growth resemble leeks or young corn. They vary considerably in size from species to species. The flowers are produced from the leaf axils and have a most unusual form for an iris. The standards are small and either horizontal or pointing downwards like stiff, narrow little wings and can be seen between the bases of the falls. The falls are either horizontal with upright enlarged crests or are held upright at an angle of 45 degrees by the stiff style arms.

I. bucharica, probably the best known and most widely grown of the Junos, is one of the easiest to cultivate, requiring only good drainage and a sunny situation. It does not need lifting in summer. Under perfect conditions, established clumps will grow up to 40 cm in height, but 20–30 cm is more usual. It is free-flowering, large bulbs producing up to eight flowers in succession. The topmost flower is the first to open followed by other flowers progressively down the stem. The standards are a creamy yellow, as are the falls, apart from the orange-yellow blade. The broad upright crests are white, as are the style arms.

An all-yellow form is grown as *I. orchioides*, which is smaller flowered and has winged falls. It is possibly a variant rather than a true species, however both plants are worthy of cultivation. The plant grown as *I. orchioides* is the last to flower in spring. Seedlings take up to five years to flower.

I. magnifica is a robust plant that is occasionally available from specialist nurseries and is quite easy to grow. It is the tallest-growing species, reaching 30–60 cm in height, with many shiny green leaves 3–5 cm wide scattered up the stem so that the internodes are visible at flowering time. The three to seven large flowers are up to 7.5 cm in diameter and are a delicate lilac with the usual yellow zone and an undissected white crest. A prominent feature of the falls is the wide wings on the haft.

I. persica is an exotic and rare species that flowers almost at ground level. The one to four flowers are quite large and have fascinating and strange colour combinations of pale greenish blue, the fall tipped with a dark purplish blotch and a golden median ridge dotted with black. These colours vary considerably.

I. 'Sindpers' is a lovely sterile hybrid between *I. aucheri* and *I. persica* that is quite widely cultivated. It grows and flowers reasonably consistently, although it tends to dwindle and die with age. This has lovely slatey sapphire flowers with an orange zone and pale green-edged falls. It is probably the loveliest of them all and sometimes flowers quite early in the winter — an added virtue, but as a result needs some protection from frosts. It only grows about 10 cm high.

I. planifolia (syn. *I. alata*) is the only European Juno species. It requires a rich well-drained soil in a position where it will get a good baking in summer and have sun at all times of the year. Most of the other species prefer a rather stiff rich loam. Plenty of lime is acceptable to *I. planifolia*, but the plant resents disturbance. It is a dwarf grower, 10–15 cm in height, with arching, shiny green foliage. The large bulbs have fleshy, but not swollen, roots. Two or three blooms are produced in succession from the top down. They are about 6–7 cm in diameter with tiny blue, horizontally held standards, the wings below the main part of the flower. The style arms hold up the falls, which then open out to a horizontal position, with the crests curving upwards like the standards of more orthodox-shaped irises. The falls are beautifully ruffled and waved, of a lovely shade of pale blue, and have a median ridge of bright orange.

I. aucheri (syn. *I. sindjarensis*) is of interest as one of the parents of *I.* 'Sindpers'. It is a tall-growing Juno with rather robust foliage for the size of the flowers. The leaves are bright green, well-developed at flowering time, and completely enclose the stem until fruiting time, when the stem elongates so that the internodes are visible. The colour of the flowers is somewhat variable, but a form with lovely pale blue flowers with a raised yellow median ridge and tiny deflexed blue standards may be met with. It is early flowering in warmer districts. If it is necessary to lift the bulbs, they should go back into the ground as soon as possible, as the plant re-roots in early autumn. The foliage appears in early winter and should be protected from heavy frosts. Up to six delicately scented flowers are produced in the leaf axils on the 15–40 cm stem. It likes loose and perhaps lighter soil than other Junos.

I. warleyensis is some 20–45 cm tall and at maturity droops rather untidily. The foliage is narrower than many of the tall Junos. The standards are very small and deflexed and the crests are elongated and upright, curving upwards in the manner of the standards of other irises. The falls are an intense reddish violet with a conspicuous orange signal on a white ground. The haft of the falls is unwinged. The flower colour varies from light to dark violet or purplish blues.

I. 'Warlsind' is a hybrid between *I. warleyensis* and *I. aucheri*. In some plants the standards are pale greeny blue, slightly streaky in colour, and the falls are bright yellow with a greenish black blade and thin jet-black stripes, three or four to each fall. Both leaves and flowers are more robust and of thicker texture than those of *I. bucharica*.

A miniature Reticulata, *I. danfordiae*

The leaves are broader and silvery with wavy edges. Not the least of its charms is that the individual flowers have the scent of a large bunch of violets.

I. willmottiana is another fine species. It is a robust but short plant about 15–25 cm in height with thickened but not swollen roots. The short stem is completely covered at flowering time by about eight broad shiny green leaves densely packed together at first but becoming less so towards the fruiting time as the stem elongates. The four to six large flowers are a lovely soft lavender or pale purple colour with blotches of white mingled with deeper lavender marks on the blade of the falls. Although the haft of the falls is winged the transition from claw to blade is gradual, not abrupt as it is, for example, in *I. persica* or *I. magnifica*. The crest is whitish, not markedly crinkled, and the standards are about 1–5 cm long, varying from nearly diamond shaped to three lobed.

Reticulata irises

These little bulbous irises give some of our brightest patches of winter colour and are unsurpassed for a rock garden, where conditions can be provided to their liking. The first of them come into flower early in the winter and different species continue the display until spring. A warm sheltered spot will give them the best chance to show the full beauty of their delicate flowers, and they show to advantage against a protective

Two *I. reticulata* forms

rock. The flowers are virtually stemless, the plant only reaching its maximum height of up to 25 cm after the flowers have withered.

The first to flower is *I. histrio*, one of the oldest cultivated plants in the world — it can be found illustrated in bas-relief on the ancient temple at Karnak. It may not be easy to obtain good, round, acclimatised bulbs, but once obtained they increase reasonably fast. *I. histrio* is known as the actor iris because of the gay yellow ridge and purple-spotted, sky-blue falls.

It is closely followed in bloom by *I. histrioides*. This iris pops through the ground almost in full flower and quite leafless. The lovely rich blue flowers against bare earth are proof that miracles do happen. A well-grown bulb will produce two or three blooms and the later flowers lighten in colour to an almost Wedgwood blue. The sturdy pointed leaves lengthen rapidly once flowering is almost over, sometimes to as much as 60 cm long, and must be treated carefully, in spite of their untidiness, as they provide the nourishment for the next year's flowers.

A miniature and obstinate relative is *I. danfordiae*, a bright and showy yellow beauty, if it can be persuaded to flower. If a bulb can be brought to flowering size — and flower — it splits up into a myriad of tiny bulblets that require infinite care and patience to nurse to flowering size again. If it can be obtained, in view of its nasty habits, plant it in sunken pots, so that you may more easily rescue the little bulblets for growing on.

Another miniature of a distinctly more accommodating nature is *I. bakeriana*. This species has sky-blue standards, navy-blue falls and white shoulders speckled with dark blue. Its early winter-flowering habit demands care in culture and protection from wintry weather and slugs. It can be grown most successfully in a pot of sandy soil sunk in the ground so that the bulbs cannot be lost. This practice also allows it to be brought inside to be enjoyed, and admired, when the flowers appear.

And so we come to *I. reticulata* itself, whose lovely little scented flowers are deep blue-violet with a bright gold stripe on the fall. In the wild, most of the forms are a rich, dark red-purple. *I. reticulata* bulbs are reasonably easy to obtain and there are some very desirable colour forms, such as 'Cantab' (china blue) and 'J.S. Dijt' (bright red-purple). There are also two lovely hybrids between *I. reticulata* and *I. histrioides*, 'Harmony' and 'Joyce', which possess the best qualities of both parents.

A more recent introduction is *I. winogradowii*, a magnificent species that is becoming more readily available. The large flowers are lemon-yellow with an orange crest and a few darker spots on the falls. It is reputedly very hardy.

Two good new hybrids are 'Katherine Hodgkin', whose flowers are a combination of sea-green, blue and sulphur-yellow; and 'Natascha', the flowers of which are an unusual ivory-white, veined green with golden yellow blotches.

All of these small irises deserve a special sheltered corner in full sun. Ordinary garden soil, somewhat sandy and containing lime, seems to suit them best. Early planting is essential, January preferably, as they produce most of their roots in autumn. However, do not expect to see them above ground until mid-winter. They should be planted as deeply as 15 cm, either in pots sunk into the ground or directly in the soil.

Pests and diseases

The best way to combat pests and diseases in the garden is to maintain a high standard of garden hygiene. This means removing and burning dead leaves and trimmings from the plants. The dying leaves of bearded irises should not be allowed to fall onto the rhizomes. If bearded irises are grown in a mixed border try to keep the more leafy plants from over-shadowing the iris rhizomes. If you can manage without sprays, so much the better, but where they must be used read the instructions carefully and carry them out exactly.

Leaf spot and aphids are the most common troubles of bearded irises. It should be sufficient to spray a couple of times in early spring with an all-purpose spray, then again before flowering. If the weather is wet and humid another spray may be needed in between.

Rust is unsightly and can attack bearded and Louisiana irises but can be effectively controlled by spraying in mid-winter with Mancozeb. Spray mainly the base of the leaves and the surrounding soil, which helps to control other diseases as well.

Soft rot is caused mainly by poor drainage, excessive nitrogen, or from dead leaves or other plants covering the rhizomes. It is recognisable by its dreadful smell. If found in time the rhizome can be dug up and the rot trimmed away, dipped in a fungicide and allowed to dry before replanting in fresh soil. If it is very bad, burn the rhizome.

Much harder to combat are crown rot and corky rot. There is no smell with these. The former is first seen when the leaves rot at the base and fall over. By this time the roots have started to rot and are often attacked by a secondary disease known as mustard seed fungus. This covers the rotting part with a grey web with small brown spots not unlike mustard seed attached to it. Very little can be done at this stage, as the centre of the rhizome will be brown and spongy. If any part of the rhizome can be found that is not infected, try the same treatment as for soft rot, otherwise it should be destroyed. Corky rot is similar but does not attract the mustard seed fungus. The rhizome just turns brown and shrivels up. The plant looks sickly and stunted and often the tips of the leaves turn red-brown. The best way to combat these diseases is to prevent their appearance through strict garden hygiene.

If re-planting irises in the same bed, be very careful not to leave old roots behind to rot. A spade is not a good tool for lifting irises; a fork is far better, as it brings out all the roots intact.

Opposite: *I. unguicularis* 'Mary Barnard'

If you are troubled with any of these diseases it is a good idea to fumigate the bed at planting time. It is not difficult and your irises will come to no harm in the three weeks it takes if they are spread out in the shade. Read the instructions carefully and make certain you have good black plastic, with no holes, to cover the bed and bricks to weight it down. If the fumigated bed is not kept airtight it is a wasted effort and can have a very detrimental effect on the irises. When the plastic is removed it pays to give the bed a good soaking before replanting. Dig the bed over to aerate the soil and leave for two to three weeks to make sure all gas has dissipated.

Most irises are comparatively free of disease, although some are susceptible to a fungal infection caused through weather and soil conditions. The symptoms are leaves turning brown and rotting at the base. The Pacific Coast irises are the most likely to be attacked and it has been found that growing plants from seed and planting them out while still small gives a better success rate than dividing plants. When planting out seedlings it pays to dip them in fungicide and drench the bed with the same mixture. If only part of the plant is attacked they can sometimes be saved by cutting out the infected part and thoroughly drenching the remaining plant and soil around it with a fungicide. Repeat in three weeks and again in three months. Be sure to burn all infected parts and remember that the soil where the plant was growing, unless fumigated, may still retain the disease spores. Siberians, Spurias and *I. unguicularis* are very occasionally attacked, usually if growing in soil that is badly drained. Also avoid watering in the heat of the day, especially with the Pacific Coast irises and the Spurias, which prefer to be fairly dry in summer.

Irises are also susceptible to viruses, which are spread by aphids or dirty tools. They are usually evident once the leaves emerge or at flowering, but some viruses have little or no effect on the plant. The leaves are streaked with yellow and rot at the base, or the flowers are deformed or mottled. Infected bulbous irises may fail to flower. There is absolutely no cure and the bulbs must be dug up and burnt. If possible, fumigate the bed. The bearded iris virus lies dormant in most bearded forms and if the plant is grown under good conditions never shows up. But if the plant is not happy and is retarded in its growth and shows yellow streaking on the leaves it should be moved to new soil with good drainage and plenty of sun and given all the feeding it requires. If the plant does not respond it is better to discard it, as it is probably very badly infected.

Irises are occasionally attacked in a wet season by bacterial leaf spot, which is easily distinguished by brown to black spots or streaks on the leaves. A general rose spray should deal with the leaf spot, along with any aphids, which are rather fond of the bulbous irises. Good hygiene is also important.

Slugs and snails can severely damage the buds and flowers, but may also rasp the foliage. Thick clumps provide an ideal hiding place for these pests. Scattering slug bait around the plants during the flowering season is therefore essential.

Propagation

In general, irises are easy to propagate and increase reasonably quickly. However, it is important to remember that named forms must only be propagated vegetatively (that is, by division), as none will be true-breeding from seed — the seedlings will be variable and not identical to the parent. In addition, some hybrids are sterile and do not set viable seed, so division is the only means by which gardeners can propagate such plants. Species will come true from seed as long as cross-pollination with a compatible species or cultivar does not occur; to ensure this does not happen self-pollination by hand may be advisable.

Division

Rhizomatous irises are propagated by dividing the clump into individual rhizomes. Bearded irises, Talls and Medians alike, should be divided every three to four years, or sooner if they become overcrowded and bloom less. This is best done six weeks after flowering has finished and no later than the end of February.

The whole clump should be lifted with a fork. The two fans either side of the spent bloom stalk are most likely to flower in the following season. Use a sharp knife to cut off all the fresh rhizomes, discard the old ones, retaining only the newest for replanting. Trim the old roots and, using sharp shears, cut back the fan of leaves by at least half. The smaller dwarf varieties are easier to handle if kept in small clumps and not cut down to individual rhizomes. Bearded irises can be kept in a cool, dry spot, say under trees, for two to three weeks while the bed is being remade. Replant in groups of four to five rhizomes in a circle or triangle to allow for increase, leaving sufficient space so they will not grow into one another. Barely cover the rhizome with soil to prevent sunburn or frost damage and water in until the roots have become established and the plant feels firm.

Siberian irises can be left to make good-sized clumps and should never be broken into small pieces. Back-to-back forks can be used to separate clumps.

Pacific Coast irises can be divided only when new fat white roots are present in spring or after autumn rains, and it is best to lift only part of the clump.

Bulbous irises are easily divided while dormant by removing the small offset bulbs (or bulbils) that develop around the base of the original bulb. These can be grown on but will usually take two or three years to flower, depending on their original size.

Growing irises from seed

Iris seed contains an inbuilt inhibitor against germination. It is nature's way of guarding against premature growth in unsuitable conditions. The drier the seed becomes, the harder it is to break down this inhibitor. It is generally accepted that the fresher the seed when planted, the higher will be the percentage of germination. Seed harvested from the gardener's own irises should be shelled when the pod begins to split and placed in an open container to dry out. This may be planted as soon as they are ripened. Bearded irises, if planted by mid-autumn, may bloom in eighteen months, the following spring.

Seed of beardless species that are naturally dormant in winter are often best left until late winter to be planted, to avoid seedlings being killed off in frosty weather. Store these in an airtight container with a dusting of fungicide. There are many recipes for breaking down the anti-germination substance but the most simple is to soak the seed in water, at least overnight, or even several days before planting. Change the water several times in this case.

Seed can be sown in trays or pots; the open ground is not recommended for irises. Germination will still be erratic, and it is simpler to keep track of individual varieties in a pot. Pots may be sunk in the ground to prevent their drying out. They can be placed in a semi-shaded spot or in a cold frame. If the latter is used, be sure the ventilation is adequate, and it is advisable to dust the seeds before planting with a fungicide to prevent damping off. Note that heated glasshouses are not suitable.

For the growing medium, a commercial seed-raising mix can be used, but be careful it does not become too wet. A suitable mix is half coarse river sand and half peat, with a little liquid fertiliser added. Soak the mix well before planting. Plant the seed fairly thickly, cover lightly with the mix, and add a layer of fine gravel or grit as a moss deterrent. Label the pot well and, as an extra precaution, keep a separate record in a diary. Keep the pots damp and wait patiently. Germination may not occur the first year in some of the beardless species.

Planting out should be done only when the plants are big enough to handle, four or five leaves at least. Tip the whole pot out gently onto the ground, tease out the roots of the seedlings and plant them in the prepared position. Some gardeners prefer to plant species very close together, believing that they thrive in these conditions. This has the added advantage that, as the plants reach flowering stage, they become crowded and so only the most superior ones will be kept. Random and bee-crossed seedlings should be labelled thus: '*I. siberica* seedling'; they will very likely be different from the parents.

Some of the beardless species require different handling. Japanese irises may be grown from seed by gathering the seeds as soon as they are ripe, soaking for 24 hours and then placing them in a covered container in the fridge for ten days. Sow at once and cover lightly. Protect seedlings from frost.

Arils and bulbous irises are best left in their pots until the autumn, over their summer dormant period, and planted out when growth restarts. Be particularly careful when transplanting Juno seedlings; the long, fleshy roots on the base of the bulb should not be broken. Some growers advise planting the seed of these into very deep pots and leaving them in situ for several years, feeding with blood and bone and phostrogen.

Louisianas will be more successfully grown from seed by picking off the corky outer shell of each seed before it is planted. Iris seed is viable for many years, some seed even having been recorded as germinating after eighteen years. Generally those species of irises producing the most abundant seed are those that germinate most quickly, for example the Pacific Coast and Siberian irises, *I. tectorum* or *I. setosa*. The exotic Oncocyclus species can take up to five years to germinate. For the beginner, the easier species offer a quicker return from seed to bloom.

Specialist iris nurseries

New Zealand

Bay Bloom, PO Box 502, Tauranga (bearded, Siberians)

Daffodil Acre, PO Box 834, Tauranga (Reticulatas, Junos)

Glenleigh Iris Gardens, Orion Road East, RD 6, Invercargill (Tall Beardeds, Japanese, species)

Mossburn Iris Gardens, PO Box 96, Mossburn (bearded, Spurias, Siberians)

Netherby Gardens, Mandeville, RD 6, Gore (bearded)

O'tara Birch Gardens, PO Box 81, Rongotea 5454 (Japanese, Siberians, Laevigatas, Tall Bearded, water-loving species, Louisianas, Spurias)

Otepopo Garden Nursery, Private Bag, Herbert, North Otago (species)

Piki Carroll, Te Ohanga, Black Rock Road, RD 6, Masterton (Tall Bearded, Dwarf Bearded, species)

Puketapu Iris Gardens, 226 Corbett Road, RD 3, New Plymouth (Tall and Median Bearded, Siberians, Spurias, Louisianas)

Ranch North, Clements Road, RD 3, Whangarei (Louisianas)

Rainbow Ridge™ , RD 8, Hamilton (Tall, Median and Dwarf Bearded, Louisiana, Siberian, water iris, Spuria, Japanese)

Richmond Iris Garden, 376 Hill Street, Richmond, Nelson (Tall, Median and Dwarf Bearded, Louisianas)

Waimate Iris Garden, 4 Durham Street, Waimate (Tall and Median Bearded)

North America, The British Isles & Europe

Information on plant sources may be found in the current editions of the following books:

North America
The Anderson Horticultural Library's Source List of Plants and Seeds. Chanhassen: Minnesota Landscape Arboretum.
Gardening by Mail and *Taylor's Guide to Specialty Nurseries*, by Barbara J Barton. New York; Houghton Mifflin.

British Isles
The Plant Finder. London: Royal Horticultural Society.

Europe
PPP Index: European Plantfinder, by Anne Erhardt & Walter Erhardt. Ashbourne, Derbyshire: Moorland.

Conversion charts

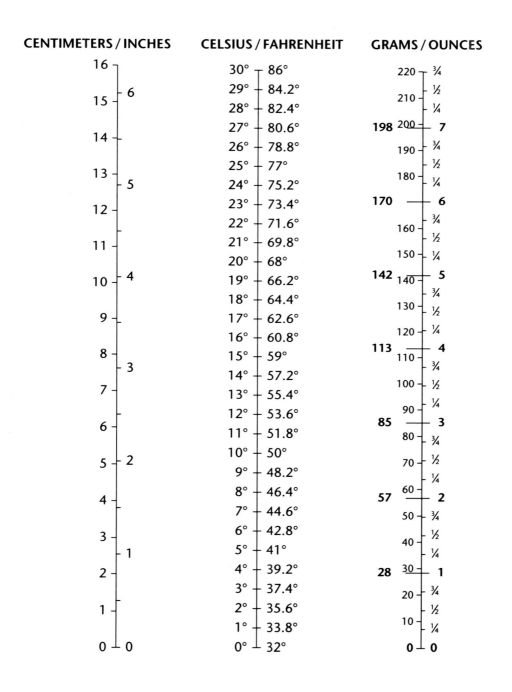

CENTIMETERS / INCHES	CELSIUS / FAHRENHEIT	GRAMS / OUNCES

CENTIMETERS / INCHES

cm	inches
16	
15	6
14	
13	5
12	
11	
10	4
9	
8	3
7	
6	
5	2
4	
3	
2	1
1	
0	0

CELSIUS / FAHRENHEIT

°C	°F
30°	86°
29°	84.2°
28°	82.4°
27°	80.6°
26°	78.8°
25°	77°
24°	75.2°
23°	73.4°
22°	71.6°
21°	69.8°
20°	68°
19°	66.2°
18°	64.4°
17°	62.6°
16°	60.8°
15°	59°
14°	57.2°
13°	55.4°
12°	53.6°
11°	51.8°
10°	50°
9°	48.2°
8°	46.4°
7°	44.6°
6°	42.8°
5°	41°
4°	39.2°
3°	37.4°
2°	35.6°
1°	33.8°
0°	32°

GRAMS / OUNCES

grams	ounces
220	¾
210	½
	¼
198 200	7
190	¾
	½
180	¼
170	6
160	¾
	½
150	¼
142 140	5
	¾
130	½
120	¼
113 110	4
	¾
100	½
90	¼
85 90	3
80	¾
70	½
	¼
57 60	2
50	¾
40	½
	¼
28 30	1
20	¾
	½
10	¼
0	0

Index

Page numbers in **bold** refer to illustrations.